MARK HA...

The Comeback Kid

The Comeback Kid

Mark Hastings

The Comeback Kid by Mark Hastings

Copyright © 2023 by Mark Hastings

All rights reserved. Under International Copyright Law, no part of this publication may be reproduced, stored, or transmitted by any means – electronic, mechanical, photographic (photocopy), recording, or otherwise – without written permission from the Publisher.

ISBN: 978-1-938082-45-0 (Paperback)
       978-1-938082-46-7 (eBook)

Published by:

Zeloo Media
Tarpon Springs, FL 34688
USA

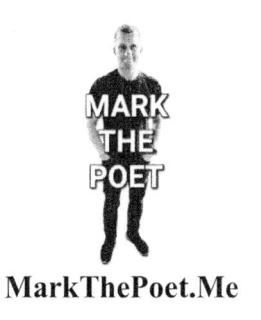

MarkThePoet.Me

In memory of my Dad

David William George Hastings
6th January, 1949 – 8th December, 2022

You will always be with me,
and you will continue
to inspire me every day.

Love you,
Dad.

World's Best Dad

There was no one like my Dad...
there is no one like my Dad,
and there never will be anyone like him...
my Dad was the kindest,
my Dad was the most giving,
my Dad was the most generous,
my Dad was the most loving man there ever was,
and because of who he was
those who were fortunate to know him
and to have met him could never forget him...
my Dad was one of a kind...
my Dad was always thinking about others
and doing things for others...
my Dad had the most amazing smile
and he had the most hypnotizing
and the most beautiful bright-blue eyes...
my Dad woke up every morning,
he looked out his bedroom window
as the sun began to rise,
and though at times it was a struggle for him
because of what life had put him through,
he got up and put one foot in front of the other
and he effortlessly was the best friend,
the best brother, the best husband,
the best father the world has ever known...
my Dad was there for me all my life...
my Dad will always be my greatest
source of inspiration, strength,
and he will always be my hero...

my Dad and I shared so much together –
but I would give anything
to have more time with him,
to do more things with him,
to talk to him and to hear him say to me:
"Do your best" –
which was something
that he used to say to me
and which will always stay with me
every day from morning till night...
life will never be the same again,
but not a day will go by when
I will not think of my Dad,
when I will not miss my Dad,
when I will not love my Dad,
when I will not do my best for my Dad;
but, to be honest, I know, and I can feel,
that he is still with me, that he is still with us –
because he was the best man there ever was
and I am the luckiest son ever
to have had the world's best Dad.

Tatters

When you grow up with nothing
you really do appreciate everything –
however, everybody always has something,
everybody always has someone,
everybody always has moments that they look back on
and people from their life that stand out
because they had a profound effect on them...
when some people are born
they are surrounded by shiny things –
but sometimes little to no love to be found.
When some people are born
they do not know that in comparison
to other people of the same age
their parents do not have the same means
to give them what other children have –
but it doesn't matter because what they have
and what they will always have is
a connection, a bond, a hidden but important
history and a tapestry that only they know.

When we want to discover more about ourselves
we look in, we look out, we look back –
just like astronomers looking up to
the starlit sky of the cosmos and the infinity of space
and the wonders to be revealed –
and we try to recapture times,
experiences, relationships, feelings;
but once something has happened
it is always hard to see and to recount
every detail of everything,
because our own internal storyteller
has a way of dramatizing and often
romanticizing things in such a way
to make them seem better or worse than they were.

When a person lives their life
they always discard pieces of themselves
that they have collected and acquired over the years –
fingerprints that could be used to identify them,
such as: messages, photographs, souvenirs, memories –
things that though they may have wanted to lose,
they kept a hold of because they still felt a longing to return
to the same place and the same time, with the same people,
they once visited, and loved, and might still love.

When someone's world implodes
there are always fragments of them
and the world that they knew
strewn in every direction
and left for others to come along
and pick up afterwards and continue
their journey in some way –
such as incorporating them into a story,
or repurposing them and recycling them
so that they can be used over and over again –
and all my life I have witnessed this
and I see the value in using what others
no long have a reason to keep,
and now that I am older, and I fully understand
what in life truly matters,
I know what it means to take the bits
and the pieces of other people's lives
and fold them into our own,
because there is so much to be learned
from picking up seemingly random things
and putting together a new puzzle –
especially to those who are adept
at using their imagination and creating new stories
from the tatters of others.

Continue on

Everything has an end date...
Everyone has an end fate...
Everything deteriorates over time...
Everyone, no matter how long they live,
only has a relatively short life.
Everything has a use...
Everyone has a path...
Everything has an expected way to be used...
Everyone has a first and a last.
Everything can be lost,
and sometimes things can be forgotten.
Everyone is human and is connected
to everybody else
and there are times when, to some people,
we are all important.
Everything is influenced by everyone
who interacts with them.
Everyone is an example of what is
necessary to remember every day –
that our time here on Earth with
those nearest and dearest to us is temporary,
so the memories that we make
should be captured in every way that we can.
Everything only means something
when someone gives it an identity that stays with people
that even after an attempt at reinvention they cannot lose.
Everyone can be someone's Everything –
but because the spirit of someone
is deeper and more complex than something,
people cannot easily be moved on from –
because the echo, the shadow, the aura
of whom they are, who they were,
and who they will always be
will continue on.

The Time is Now

It's 3 A.M. again...
it's the time of after and before...
it's quiet – which means it is
the perfect time to listen...
it is now when people like me
awaken in the dark after being
awoken to think more upon
what our inner self wishes to explore.

It is not a time suited for everybody...
it is not a time when that many
might wish to converse;
however, in my experience, it is a fertile time
to walk through the garden of poetry and inspiration –
because it is a time when the mind of everyone,
especially a poet, is open to more than they might think...
it is time to let your thoughts wander clearly
without the expectation that you might find yourself
leaping from one extreme scenario to another
like you might during a dream.

It is before the sun has risen
when I have repeatedly found myself
considering where I am, why, and how?
It is while the moon is still in the sky
when I have ventured to answer
the question: where do I go from here?

It is after leaving behind
the fog of the dream-world
that I try and recapture
something that I may have
discovered while traversing
my own internal ocean –
that is both of my own making
but is also connected
to something a great deal
more vast and deep.

It is now when I have
always been more aware
of whom and what surrounds
me and defines me –
and I believe that
for the rest of my life
it will always be
this time when
multiple realities
will continue to meet,
and whether consciously,
or not, decide that
the time is now
to reveal themselves
to me.

World Between Worlds

There is a line between darkness and light...
There is a state of mind between
hope and fear...
There is a place where both love and sadness reside...
There is a world within where we all
wear our inner smiles,
and where we all shed our hidden tears.

There is a reason for what we do
that sometimes only we know...
There is a mirror version of ourselves
who tells us what is real rather than
what we think is true...
There is an endless kaleidoscope
of memories and thoughts from our life
that when we dream we go to...
There is a path that people choose to take
when they feel as if they have nothing left to lose.

There is a balance that we all need to find...
There is a cause that we all rally around
because it means more to us
than could be captured with words...
There is a story that only we can tell –
and by the act of sharing
that which we have lived through
the truth shines and eventually parts
the clouds of deception and lies...
There is something and someone
important to us that we cling to
whenever, and wherever,
we know that we are somewhere
that is a world between worlds.

The Touch of the Poet

We can all be touched by someone...
we can all touch someone physically
as well as emotionally;
but there is no touch
like the touch of a poet
to conjure thoughts and feelings
unrivaled by any other.

The touch of a poet
is one of spellbinding magic...
the touch of a poet
is one capable of inspiring another
with ideas they may not
have thought of before...
the touch of a poet
is one that can impact more
and delve deeper –
though the time and the pressure
that a poet exerts may only be tender.

The touch of a poet
is one that is unforgettable...
the touch of a poet
is one that is unbelievable...
the touch of a poet
is one that is undeniable.

The touch of the poet
is one that connects
the world of fantasy
to the world of reality...
the touch of the poet can mean more
than any previous touch that someone
may have had before they were
impressed by the embrace
of the poet's multi-faceted poetry...
the touch of the poet can turn lust into love...
the touch of the poet is one that you can
take into your heart,
connect to your soul,
and always trust.

Whether people know it, or not,
everybody alive has
at one time or another
looked into the eyes,
has been in the presence,
has been given the gift of the words
that have the power to influence,
to transform, to embolden,
to dream, to make someone's heart
beat so fast that they
have to catch their breath –
and that is the indelible
touch of the poet.

The World Beyond

The world can change
for all of us very quickly...
the world we always knew
can seem something and somewhere different
when something unexpected happens...
the world can be many things
to many people beyond what can be seen...
the world we have always been familiar with
can always have layers to it that can lead
to a world within that has a music to it that,
when the time is right, you can hear
when you choose to listen.

The world does not end below our feet,
nor above our head...
the world is sometimes only seen
for what it truly is when we look
but do not think...
the world does not rest...
the world is everything that has happened,
everything that will happen,
and everything that we can only dream of
when we blink.

The world is bigger than can be imagined...
the world is to what we all are bound...
the world is what we receive messages from
and it is to whom our wishes are sent...
the world is growing rapidly every day,
and though the world will never be
as we want it to be
there will always be more
than our eyes can show us –
because there will always be a world beyond.

In Their Own Words

Words are powerful...
Words are meaningful...
Words can only have their required impact
when they are used in combination
with other words that interlock
either side of them in a sentence...
Words can be the key to deciphering
a particular reference...
Words can only mean what they do
when they have lived a life of interchangeability...
Words are used in unison with sounds and images
when we dream or when we wish to
convey a thought, an idea, a message to those
close, far, intentionally, or accidentally.

We can find words... We can lose words...
We can adopt words... We can save words...
We can build a world and a life with words...
We can watch someone be brought to their knees with words –
because words have a weight to them,
words have a gravity to them; words have a way about them
that when evoked in a certain way,
and when enunciated in a particular fashion
by a diction-endowed individual,
can open minds, ears, eyes, mouths,
to such a degree that allows for
the continuance of language, in all its forms,
throughout the infinite universes that harbor
many different worlds, many different sunrises,
many different communicators, authors,
dreamers, artists, writers, poets
capable of telling their own story –
but only in their own words.

In store

I used to love watching sunrises and sunsets –
but now, whenever I see one,
all I can think about
is how many more I will get to enjoy,
and how much time I have left.
Time was always something
that I thought I had a lot of…
time with people was something
that I foolishly took for granted –
then I was physically and emotionally
struck by a loss so overwhelming
that my entire attitude towards life
and what was important was impacted.

Some things hit you hard,
but you learn to recover from them...
some things knock you off your stride,
but you can relearn how to walk again...
some things you can stop doing
but you can resume at a later date.
However, there are some things –
like seeing the face of someone
who you love who you have lost –
that you know you might have to
hold on to for a long time,
because if you want to see someone again
you might have to wait,
and, most importantly,
you might have to hold on
to something even more
valuable and precious: your faith.

Over the course of a life
everybody finds someone
and something to believe in...
from beginning to end
everybody's life is a story
that has so much detail to it
that even if you tried
you would not be able to recall,
nor capture, everything...
when you wake up every morning
it can take a while to remember
who you are, where, and what happened –
even the events of the night before...
when everybody goes to bed at night –
but before they dream the night away –
there is a time that feels like you are
watching a tide rise that you are unable
to stop looking at and cannot walk away from
because what is coming towards you
is a force of the universe
that reminds us of where we came from,
where we have been, where we are going,
and somewhere that only those
who perceive time non-linearly
know for sure
what is ultimately in store.

Burst

Just like a solar storm
on the surface of the sun,
just like the fiery curls
that the sun releases
and sends out into space,
just like the auroras created
when the energy of the sun
touches the atmosphere of our planet –
everyone and everything capable
of complex thoughts, feelings, and emotions
often feels as if they have something
within them that they struggle to contain,
that they struggle to hold back,
that they struggle not to express –
because we are all filled with a spirit
that burns like a flame,
that boils like hot water,
that sometimes explodes
like a jet from a geyser.

Everyone and everything
needs at outlet to get out
what has found its way within:
whether that is artistically, physically, audibly,
or a combination of many things all at once –
because if someone or something
has no means of controlled release
then they might remark
that they will figuratively,
or perhaps literally,
BURST!

Keep on loving

We learn to love
from the moment that we are born,
from the moment that we
open our eyes for the first time
and we see the face of the one
who gave us the gift of life...
we learn what love is as our thoughts,
feelings, and our emotions blossom
and develop to a point where we know
what we want and who makes us
feel what we have always wanted to feel.

We learn what it is like to feel
as if our heart has been physically
ripped out of our chest
when our heart is broken,
when we feel like we will never recover
after someone who we cared deeply for
decided, for whatever reason,
to go their own way and say goodbye.

We learn what it is like to feel renewed,
to feel reinvigorated,
and to have been given a reinfusion of hope
when we find someone and,
from the moment that we see them,
we fall in love and we believe
that we know them
just as much as they know us –
and that from that first look, that first touch,
what you share will be forever –
but the truth is if you genuinely want to know someone
sometimes it can take a while.

We learn when to say some things
and when it is not necessary to say
anything at all when we spend more
and more time with someone
and we develop an almost psychic
bond that goes beyond the sound of our voice...
we learn that sometimes we are compelled
to do things because of how we feel
that can manifest in actions
beyond even our own understanding...
we learn that when we say
"I love you" to someone
sometimes it is because
we do not have a choice...
we learn that sometimes in life
we all have to sacrifice
something to someone –
because, by doing so,
our actions show
that when it comes to being in love
we will do whatever
it takes to be loved
and to keep on loving.

Rise to the Occasion

Life constantly teaches us new lessons...
Life never stops posing questions...
Life has a way of showing us
just how much we do not know
about ourselves and about how
we will react when we are tested...
Life gives us what we need, who we need,
to complete various activities –
sometimes in the form of memories, recollections,
and experiences that we have accumulated;
however, there comes a time in our life
when we must all step out of our comfort zone
and step into a reality that may
come to define the rest of our lives.

My life was completely and irrevocably
changed when my Dad died...
my life was thrown off course
from the moment that I realized
nothing was ever going to be the same again...
my heart, my soul, my world
was shattered beyond repair
from the moment that I felt as if
a shard of the mirror of self-reflection
became impaled within my mind...
my life was darkened from the instant
that I knew I was going to be scarred
by a pain that would never go away.

Every day, for as long as I can remember,
I have been taking the steps and walking
the path that I needed to walk
so that I may give as much as I could
to those who needed it...
every day, for as long as I have been on
my new life's mission,
I have marched like a soldier
and done what had to be done...
every day, and for all the days ahead,
I am keenly aware that the architect
of what lies over the horizon
will ask of me to be ready for whatever peak
towards which I may need to make an ascent...
every day, I wish that I could go back
and change something that has happened,
armed with the gift of hindsight –
but, because no one can ever know
exactly what will happen until it happens,
all that any of us can do when asked,
and when given a choice to act,
is to do our absolute best
as we keep going,
keep climbing,
and keep rising
to the occasion.

Always With Me

Every day, I climb the hill
to stand alongside, to speak to,
and to hear the voice of my Dad –
as I always have, and as I always will –
because my Dad will always be
the golden light that guides my way...
every day, I feel like my Dad is still with me,
because he is;
wherever I look at a photograph of my Dad
I know that he is standing alongside me,
with an arm around me,
as he whispers his lasting wish:
"Be there for those who matter the most"...
every day when I am with my Dad
the sound of birdsong can be heard all around,
and often times a robin or a pair of magpies
visits also and sing in a nearby tree,
which always makes me smile
at the same time that I start to cry...
every day, I tell my Dad I love him, and I miss him,
and I feel the touch of love
from my Dad that I always felt when I looked into his eyes,
when in my mind I felt our unique connection –
which is why I will always remember,
and why I will always reflect upon,
what my Dad did for me
and what he will always mean to me –
and even now, every day, and forever
I know more than ever that even though my Dad
may now rest atop the hill,
what made him who has was,
who he is, and who he will always be,
will always be with me
wherever I go.

Stand Up

I do my best creating while I am sitting down,
but I do my best performing when I am standing up...
when I write a poem, or a story,
I have a keyboard or a notebook in front of me;
but when I am recording something I have written
and I am talking into a microphone
I am always doing so while standing on my own two feet,
because to me there is no better way
to let out what is inside of you –
and if you do not believe me
you need only watch and listen
to a seasoned stand-up comic
who knows what it is like
to have an audience in front of them
captivated with anticipation
at what will be uttered from their mouth.

Performing in front of an audience is not easy
and it is not for everybody...
talking to others is what some people
might consider the hardest thing they have to do...
some people are extroverts
and being the centre of attention
is like being given a jolt of energy.
However, some people would rather
stay out of the limelight, in the background,
and remain hidden from view.

With practice, I have learned
to use my senses to filter out the inconsequential
and focus on what matters the most...
with repetition, I have come to understand
the best way to communicate
what it is that I want to say
and to do it with no other voice than my own...
with a saved lexicon of
language and life experience
I can convey my thoughts –
but sometimes even my own
internal dictionary
is not capable of finding a way
to describe everything,
because sometimes words are not enough...
with confidence, which can sometimes
only be found after a long time of looking,
I believe that everybody can find a way
to become more than they
ever imagined they could be
and deliver their own form of magic –
whether they are sitting down
or whether they are standing up,
delivering jokes, telling stories,
or reciting verses of poetry.

Flight Mode

Almost as soon as they break through the clouds,
the passengers and the crew members of every aircraft
immediately go into "Flight Mode" –
during which most electronic devices
do not receive, nor are supposed to transmit,
any kind of radio signals other than those necessary to help
the captain and the pilot know
what it is that they need to know...
almost as soon as a passenger jet has reached its optimal altitude
is when the onboard experience
of most modern commercial flights begin –
including the enjoyment of
whatever entertainment is available,
as well as whatever food and drink
there is to be ordered and consumed –
and, before long, the time to your destination seems to fly by
and so much so that you wonder
where all the time goes.

While flying anywhere in the world
you can find yourself sitting in front,
behind, and alongside people
you may never have met before,
and after your flight you may never see again...
while flying anywhere in the world
you can look out of the windows of the cockpit
and find yourself flying over countries
that might have their own distinct culture and language,
but when seen from above it can be hard to differentiate
one country and its people from another –
because while in the air
the world can look as if it is,
as it should be seen as being,
one and the same.

Since the very beginning
of intercontinental and international travel
it has become increasingly easier
for almost anybody to go
anywhere in the world –
especially since the ability
to be able to book a flight
and to go on holiday
has become even more accessible
and accepted than ever before –
meaning that more people now
than at any other time
can choose to go anywhere and do anything
that their heart desires and then return home
with stories of places, people,
and experiences that they have had,
as well as with souvenirs of where they have been
to share and to show.

Flying is such a normal activity
for most people to be able to do
in this day and age, that almost as soon
as some people arrive from their getaway somewhere
they are already looking in the direction
of the departures lounge of the airport
they have just flown into
and cannot wait to return to where they have been
so that they can once again
turn on their "Flight Mode."

Hola!

Hola! Hello! Hi!
Whether it is morning,
afternoon, or at night,
people greet each other
and reconnect with one another
to continue the experience of
synchronicity through communication,
by opening and closing their eyes
and by opening and closing their mouths –
sometimes voluntarily,
sometimes because it is expected,
sometimes because certain actions
over time can become rituals,
sometimes because if certain
cultural norms are not met
people can be easily offended.

The value of something
and what something costs matters
a great deal to some people...
a single word, a gesture, a look,
a smile, a touch, can go a long way...
a memory, a thought, a consideration
for someone else can mean the world...
a message from someone special to us
can make our entire day.

There are countless instances
over the course of our life
when subtleties leave a more lasting
impression than those that might be
considered more grandeur in size...
the best way to tell whether someone's
intentions are honest and selfless
is always to look into their eyes...
there have been thousands of languages
invented since the dawn of humanity,
when a small group used to look up
to the sky and dream, wonder,
worship, and ask for answers.

Whenever you find yourself
in a place you do not know well
it is always helpful and customary
to learn some of the "local lingo" –
and while on holiday recently
that is exactly what I tried to do;
however, since I have come back,
I have found myself having to hold back
from saying the word *"hola"* -
Why? Because for days on end
I used that word repeatedly,
more times than you can know,
to greet whomever I came into contact with,
and now I must retrain my brain
to revert once again
to saying a simple *"hello"*.

Vamos!

There is really no time like the present...
the past anchors us but can sometimes
seem closer or farther away than it appears...
nothing and no one stays the same for long –
explosions of energy and light burn brightly
and then return to where they came from,
but can be captured for all eternity
through the aperture of a camera lens...
the future is a constantly unveiling tapestry
that can only be quantified
when it is divided into seconds, minutes,
hours, weeks, months, and years.

The speed of light is fast –
but, even in space, there are limits...
the sound of someone's voice
can continue to be heard
long after they have passed...
there are times when we have to sacrifice
moments spent with people,
because sometimes the time we are given
isn't enough to fit everything
that we need to do in...
whether it is the footprints on The Moon,
or the tire tracks on the surface of Mars,
everyone and everything leaves impressions –
and some things endure
not just because they exist within a vacuum,
but because they are an example
of why some things
are innately meant to last.

We leave so much behind...
we all wish that we could revisit
some of the highlights from our life
and speak to some of the people
who we have lost...
we all dream of things and people
that seem to come out of nowhere –
but when it comes to our connection
with all things, everywhere,
there is no such thing as the passage of time...
when we realize that our time is short,
in comparison to most things in the universe,
we all conclude
that we need to do what we can,
where we can, when we can –
because, if we do not,
then there may come a day
when we awaken, wonder, and wish
that when we were given the chance
to do something extraordinary we had –
because so many great leaps
into the unknown started
with someone saying:
"Let's go!"

Carnival

A celebration of life...
a rainbow of colour...
an explosion of light...
a parade of wonder...
a celebration of individuality,
as well to show
that we are all one,
the same, together...
an experience that seems
dream-like when you are
in the middle of it...
a gathering of people,
unlike any other...
an atmosphere of energy
that creates something
that feels special,
which can reinvigorate
any and every spirit...
a feeling that influences
the way that people think,
speak, see, hear, and act...
a power and a natural magic
that is wonderful and unfathomable...
a way of being that people crave
and wish would always last...
a festival of love, unity,
as well as so much more
of what makes the world and existence
on this planet worth living for –
that is the heart and the soul
of a carnival.

Sustaining Truth

Every holiday celebrated
around the world
means different things
to different people...
everyone has an affinity
for some celebrations
more than most...
Easter, for example, is a time when
people young and old
get to share gifts of all sorts –
from chocolate eggs,
to traditions that for generations
have been passed down
and practiced because their message
has always been so meaningful...
the message of Easter, to me,
is that salvation can be found
by those who sometimes feel lost.

Every season has symbols
that embolize them...
every morning and evening
shares a vision of light
that is heavens sent...
every now and again
we are all asked to do
without something
to understand its essence –
like at the time of Lent.

Every faith rose and was inspired
and influenced by all others,
since our ancestors began to
worship and give names to
the constellations of the stars
of the night sky...
every way to live on Earth
has its own lessons
and its followers have their
own trials to go through...
everything that happens in life
must be accepted
and sometimes weathered –
just like a boat must ride
the infinite number of ocean waves
that are like ripples in the fabric of time...
every holiday has a reason to be embraced –
because humanity has always relied
upon the continued stories,
the ongoing mysteries,
and the significant figureheads
that are at the core of their
sustaining truth.

Walk The Walk

Some people say that they are going to do something,
but they never do...
some people say that they are going to be somewhere,
but they never are...
some people make promises
to make something happen,
but they never make the right moves...
some people say that they
are going to make a difference
but they never make their mark.

Talking about something is good...
dreaming about something is wonderful...
one drop of anything can
eventually lead to an epic flood...
believing that someone will be there
for you when you need them is great,
because it is necessary in life
to trust and to have faith in people.

Not everything can happen how we want it to...
sometimes some people are, unfortunately, all talk...
not everybody is as forthcoming
about their intentions and motivations,
and sometimes someone who we thought would never change
can surprise us by doing something
we never thought they would do...
in my experience, when you can,
you should always endeavor to
be a person of your word,
and when you need to, if you are able,
if you are going to talk the talk
make sure that you also
walk the walk.

42

Today is the day...
Today is the time I have been
waiting for...
Today is the end and the beginning
of a brand-new age...
Today is my birthday,
but not just any birthday:
this birthday feels unlike every other
that has come before –
it feels as if I have reached
the summit of a mountain
and I am looking out
to the landscape of my life
and everything and everyone,
who once seemed so close,
now seem so far away.

Today, more so than at any other time,
when I look back and I remember
who I have known and where I have been,
I realize just how much I have lost...
Today, more than I could ever describe,
when I look in the mirror
or when I look at photos from the past,
I see the choices that I have taken
that have changed me and molded me
into the man I am...
Today, more than yesterday,
when I return to places I know well,
I see flashes of faces and experiences
that appear as if made up of fragments of dust...
Today, looking forwards, I know that
things will never be the same again.

Today, I have the ability
to see behind,
as well as to see beyond...
Today, I have the instinct to do
what I always want to do:
to go with the flow
and to not worry about anything,
and to act as if I have nothing left to lose...
Today, as always, I am grateful
for my family, for my friends,
for those who have
given me the keys of inspiration
that I use every day to open up
the door of perception and imagination...
Today, I celebrate
finally reaching the age
that is the same
as my favourite number
and the answer to life,
the universe, and everything:
yes, today I am
42.

Millennium

In a thousand years
what will be left?
In a thousand years
what will be left of us?
In a thousand years
what will be left of our planet?
In a thousand years
what will be uncovered
underneath the dust?
In a thousand years
what will we be thanked for
by future generations?
In a thousand years
what will we as a species look like?
In a thousand years
will everyone be a cybernetic organism?
In a thousand years
will people have to stay inside
most of the time to shield
from the intensity of the sun's light?
In a thousand years
will humanity
be living on other worlds,
and travelling through time,
as well as through space?
In a thousand years
will we have forgotten
what we now hold most dear?

In a thousand years
will we have been contacted
by multiple intergalactic
inhabitants of the galaxy,
not mention the universe?
In a thousand years
will people worship
Artificial Intelligence
and think of them as
all-knowing electronic gods?
In a thousand years
will we have created a source
of universal equilibrium?
In a thousand years
will we wish then that we now
would have learned our lessons
about tempting fate?
Only our descendants
can know for sure
what is going to happen
in the thousand years
of the next millennium.

Life's Light

Energy can neither be created nor destroyed,
but energy can change form...
the creation of all things began
billions of years ago,
but nothing is as it was...
people can be emotionally open
and then transition into becoming closed off –
even doors can change
into becoming walls...
you can prepare for the rest of your life,
but what no one can ever be ready for
is the end of days that follows
a particularly painful absence and loss.

Endings are necessary.
Full stops are essential.
Severance hurts,
but sometimes it can also
be seen as an opportunity.
Everything big
over time transitions back
into becoming small.

Generations leave legacies...
life needs regeneration...
love is a dream...
to march, every army of ideas
needs the beat of a resounding drum...
time is precious beyond belief...
every day needs a night...
the world is not all that we see...
every exposure is a convergence
and a prism of the fundamental
colours of what makes life's light.

Out of your shell

It is good to challenge ourselves...
it is good to take on new responsibilities...
it is good to do things
we have never done before –
in fact, it is essential in maintaining
our mental health...
it is good to expand our knowledge,
see the sights and meet new people
from different localities...
it is good to be immersed
in the unfamiliar...
it is good to test our tolerances...
it is good to let down our guard
and converse with people
who have different answers
to the question: why are we here?
it is good not to worry
about if someone is watching
and just do your thing –
even if it leads to you involuntarily
making a joke, singing, or starting to dance...
it is good to look the way you want to look...
it is good to have your own opinion
of what is beautiful...
it is good to have an imagination
and to have the gift to be able
to see the faces and to hear the voices
of characters that you read in a book...
it is good to step out of your comfort zone
and embrace the opportunity
to be able to fly free of your nest
and naturally find yourself
coming out of your shell.

Writer's High

That spark! That flash!
That light from the dark...
That stream of inspiration
and energy that flows so fast...
That moment of conception...
That shockwave and expansion
of the internal explosion...
That rush to capture that which
you know is significant...
That immediate change
that runs rampant like a fire
and effects everything
like a solar flare from the Sun...
That pulse-racing, breathtaking,
eye-opening idea that comes
to an artist seemingly from out of nowhere –
like a bolt from out of the blue –
can feel like a miracle from heaven
or from a higher dimension –
because the colours that it paints the world with
can seem too incredible to be real...
when an artist who uses words to create their art
feels themselves being pulled along
by an idea's wave and riptide
they can experience an almost
inconceivable soul-fulfilling ascension
that might be described
as a "writer's high".

Mad Rush

During the hours and the days
of November and December,
there is always this energy
in the air that can be felt
and which can intoxicate people in many ways,
and which can bring out the best in people –
love, charity, friendship, family;
however, which can also, sometimes,
bring out the worst in people –
competitiveness, jealousy, inferiority –
and it is during the Christmas period
that people behave in ways they never would
at any other time of the year.

Christmas should be a happy time
when people think about one another;
however, there are moments when some people
can become overly self-conscious
and they can believe that something
that they have must be "better"
than what everybody else has
for it to be considered "good".

November to December should be when
family is the most important
and everybody should be thankful
for whom and what they have in their life...
the "holiday season" – as it is known –
is and should be when there are literal
and poetic examples of hopefulness
and light on show from morning till night.

Every year, everybody around the world
participates in traditions and customs
that can only be practiced at a particular time,
for particular reasons, during which and because of
the meaning of different seasons –
and depending on what time of the year it is
some things are considered obligatory and a "must"...
every year everybody slowly but surely
changes their demeanor,
and sometimes people can even change the way
that they think and react to certain things –
and there are times when ordinarily calm
and collected individuals can find themselves
switching to a version of their personality
that voluntarily runs,
and sometimes even fights,
with those that are also
in the midst of the "red mist"
of the annual "mad rush".

Variety

I love to listen. I love to observe.
I love to imagine. I love to converse.
I love to watch people doing things
that they are invested in,
and I love to watch people do things
that they might not even know
what exactly they are doing.

I love stories, I love characters –
and life is full of an infinite number
of tales that, unless you were a witness to them,
you could not and would not believe
they were in fact real.
I love music for many reasons –
but mostly because music is like gravity:
it is ever-present throughout our lives,
it influences us, it grounds us,
it is a force of nature that stars of all kinds,
sizes, and colours create and sing
without even knowing it,
and because it existed before us
and it will live on after us in varying forms,
rhyming and as well as repeating.

I love that there is more than one
season of nature where I live,
because it stops every day from feeling
like a copy of the day before –
like it must feel to people
who live in a country where the weather,
the temperature, the sights, the sounds, are all the same –
because what I love and what I embrace
the most about the world that I live in
is that there is always so many sources of variety.

What You Make of It

Time is precious. Time is fast.
Time can be counted
in the things we have done,
in the things we have collected,
in the people we have met,
or perhaps in the steps that we have taken –
like those that need to be remembered
when learning a dance.

Time can be found.
Time can go missing.
Time can be filled with sound.
Time can be filled with silence –
and it is in those moments
when we all should listen.

Time can be spent doing many things.
Time is what gifts me inspiration.
Time can be perceived as being
both a curse as well as a blessing.
Time is a beginning, a journey,
an experience, as well as a destination.

Time is the when, the what, the why,
and the how we can be who we want to be.
Time can be the truth, as well as a secret.
Time is real, as well as a dream.
Time can be so encompassing
that it can make you believe
that where you are, when, and with whom
could not be any more perfect –
but Time is always open to interpretation,
because, in essence,
Time is what you make of it.

Like a Paper Bag in the Rain

Getting from place to place
is not always as easy
as a hop, a skip, and a jump...
getting what is in your mind
on to a piece of paper is sometimes
not as easy as it sounds...
getting what you want in life
is not always want is meant to happen...
getting an idea is sometimes
the first step of many that you need to take
to get the final rocket launch
of a final product off the ground...
getting help when you need it
is not always guaranteed –
however people can surprise you,
especially strangers who can see
that you might benefit from
a helping hand of their assistance...
getting reassurance from others
about what someone is doing
is essential for some people
who rely on constructive opinions,
not criticism, of their actions to fine-tune their art...
getting somewhere when the sun is shining
is always much easier to do than
attempting to get somewhere
when it is slippery, or wet.
However you find your way
through what you must go through
to make it to where you need to be,
if the end-result is worth it
then you will risk being completely
decimated, disintegrated, reborn, and reconstituted
like a proverbial paper-bag in the rain.

Stream

To me there is no better way
to get to know someone
than to talk to them...
to me there is no better way
to find commonalities with people
than to open up to someone...
to me there is no better way
to find out who each of us are
than to look at the face of another
who might seem as opposite and yet
familiar to us as our own reflection...
to me there is no better way
to lose yourself than to
allow yourself to fall in love.

Life is a much more fulfilling experience
when you choose to have a meeting of minds
with people from different walks of life...
life is always much more interesting
when you look beyond what is familiar
and you seek to see what lies
over the ever-present horizon...
life is much more entrancing to all our senses
when we choose to not deprive ourselves
of what drives us and what inspires us...
life is always more fascinating and enlightening
when you give someone the time
to hear what they have to say –
perhaps someone who may have been waiting
to tell that which has been on their mind
and on the tip of their tongue for far too long.

When you invite
someone to join you,
when you offer
someone a seat,
when you make
a connection
that might never
have happened
if you and another
had not chosen
to sit down, to talk,
and to listen –
what can follow as a result
may continue to flow
naturally
and undeterred
for days, for weeks,
perhaps even
for years to come,
between you
and someone else,
like a constantly
evolving
stream.

Write What You Like

For me writing is my passion...
For me writing is my release...
For me writing is my fashion...
For me writing is my peace...
For me writing is my voice....
For me writing is my road...
For me writing is a necessity and not a choice...
For me writing is how I can reach out
and remind others that nobody is ever alone...
For me writing is a dream made real...
For me writing is what has given me
gifts of experience of perspective
that I might never have known otherwise...
For me writing is the first thing
that I feel like doing whenever
I want to take a serene walk
through an Elysium-like countryside field,
and whenever I want to remember who I am,
or whenever I feel like I need to heal...
For me writing is to a writer
what singing is to a singer –
they have to do what they feel they must.
And just as a singer must love what they sing,
in my opinion, no matter what words
a wordsmith conjures from their imagination,
a writer should like what they write –
especially if writing is
what a writer loves.

Blood

Who I am, what I am,
what I have done,
where I have been
will always be within me...
what I have dreamed...
what I have lived through...
who I have done what I have done with
has always been, and will always be,
within every one of my stories
and within every verse of my poetry.

Nobody can go back and edit
moments from their own past...
nobody can undo what has been done...
nobody can stop time racing by too fast...
nobody can deny moments from their life
of defiance, of rebellion, of pleasure –
especially those that at a given time
were unapologetically fun.

You have the power to choose
some things in your life...
you have the gift to run
or to stay stuck in the mud...
you have the opportunity every day
to light a fire in someone else's eyes...
you have the spirit and the energy within you
to connect generations of time
by allowing your imagination to wander,
by allowing your dreams to become real,
and by interpreting the messages left
by our ancestors that will forever be
encoded within the story of our genetics
that can be found within a single drop of blood.

Expect the Unexpected

When we are children we are told what we can,
what we cannot, what we should,
and what we should not do...
even as we get older some people
do not want to give up their control
over their offspring and allow them
to walk on their own two feet
and give them the gift of trust and independence...
if people are beholden to too many restrictions
when they get the opportunity
some people will naturally rebel –
especially if they feel as if they have nothing to lose...
if people are told that plans have already
been made for them to do something,
without first being consulted,
then independently minded individuals
will give their own two cents and go their own way –
because some people do not like
having the gift of choice being taken away from them...
there is an unmistakable look in the eye
of someone who is always going to buck the trend
and not do what they are told...
there is a noticeable expression on the face
of those who say one thing,
but who are almost definitely going to do the opposite...
there is a path of past actions and transgressions
that when reflected upon
may be able to predict when, why, and how
someone will ultimately break the mold...
there is an unwritten rule
that even the most predictable, dependable,
and admittedly boring people
can at times surprise even themselves –
and that is why it is best to expect the unexpected.

Day of the Poet

I believe that every day of my life
has prepared me for who I am,
who I have always been,
and who I will always be...
I believe that every day of my life –
from the moment I wake up
in the early hours of the morning,
to the moment I fall asleep at night,
to the moment I set sail upon the waves
of the sea of my dreams –
I am seeing, hearing, thinking,
imagining, interpreting the poetry
all around me that will always continue
to invigorate me and inspire me...
I believe that every day when a word,
a verse, a story, or a new discovery
plants it's seed within my mind
it has been put there so that I can
see it become something even more profound
by giving it my own spark of magic...
I believe that every day when
I reflect inwards and outwards
I draw in and I echo from myself
something that was always meant to be
shared with those who need to hear
my message all around the world –
from Atlanta to Zurich...
I believe that every day when
I am writing something that is in every way a part of me,
as well as inspired by who I have met,
what I have done, where I have been,
and when I have been struck by inspiration,
was always preordained –
which is the reason that I never ask: why?

I believe that every day
when my heart was broken,
I believe that every day
when I was blessed
to see the sunrise,
I believe that every day
when I had to keep
my thoughts unspoken,
I believe that every day
when I told someone I loved them,
as I looked deep into their eyes –
every moment, of every hour,
of every day has always been
when it was my time
for me to be me
and to shine my poetic light,
because being a poet and a writer
is the daily destiny of my life.

Big Heart

I care about people... I care about places...
I care about things that matter to me...
I care about the people who care about me...
I care about the places that I have visited
that will always have a connection to me...
I care about the things that will always interest me,
anchor me, thrill me, and inspire me...
I have welcomed many people into
my circle of friends and I have trusted
some people as if they were family –
however, occasionally, unfortunately,
I have had my trust taken for granted...
I have found myself in places of extreme beauty
that I loved every moment of while I was there –
but, because I shared my time with others
who have over time seemingly put me on mute,
whenever I return to some places
I see and I hear echoes of the past that,
because I am who I am,
have not faded from my memory...
I have had things of mine taken away from me –
things that I have had to adapt to living without;
however, because everything of importance,
at one time or another,
always leaves an indelible impression on me
the touch of something, of somewhere,
or of someone, lingers on
and can never be banished from
the limitless world within
of my big heart.

Lost and Found

It has been a long time since I wrote like this…
It has been a long time since I felt like this…
It has been a long time since I felt as if I were adrift…
It has been a long time since I made a wish…
It has been a long time since I felt as if I had
nothing else to anchor me
except for my family and my poetry.
It has been a long time since I looked in the mirror
and I did not recognize who was looking back at me…
It has been a long time since I saw some of the muses
who over the last ten years have knowingly,
or unknowingly, inspired me.
It has been a long time since
I experienced a true new beginning –
but now that I have been left by those
who I once thought I knew and who I thought knew me,
I believe that I am having to walk while fully awake –
where before, perhaps, I had only been sleep-walking.
It has been a long time,
but I think I know who I am now…
It has been a long time,
but I think I get the message clear and loud…
It has been a long time,
but I think I have been touched by a light
like the sunlight that eventually
breaks through even the darkest of clouds…
It has been a long time,
but I think I have arrived somewhere
where I have acquired
what I have been looking for –
somewhere I can only acquaint to being
some kind of poetic
Lost and Found.

Transitional

Life is always transitioning
from one state of being to another –
but the act and the art of change
is no more apparent, prominent,
invigorating, and awe-inspiring
than at the time of the year
of when Spring becomes Autumn,
when the leaves of the trees change colour
and then ultimately let go and fall.

People are always thinking, listening,
feeling, and looking for new things,
or familiar things,
to excite or reignite their senses –
and there is no time like the present
when anybody can seemingly do anything,
when anyone can look how they want,
when anyone can be whoever and whatever they want to be.

Places are always having new visitors to them,
and there are always those people
who return to a place time after time –
because a certain place has something about it
that is special, magical,
and gets under a person's skin deeper than a needle.

In my experience, life is full of poetry...
in my experience, people are more pliable
than they think they are...
in my experience, every place has a story
that speaks volumes and can be heard
if you want to hear what it has to say...
in my experience, life experience is
what gives us all the gift of indistinguishable individuality.

In my experience, some people
can only show their best side when
everything around them is dark
and they can shine like the brightest of stars...
in my experience, we can all find ourselves
somewhere, and with someone, that can influence us,
and who we can in turn have an influence on,
the more that we are exposed to them –
especially if we are with someone,
somewhere, almost every day.

Life does not always give everybody a choice
as to whether they want to change or not –
because sometimes
some things must happen,
whether we want them to happen or not...
life has moving pieces and things
that must repeat and work
in synchronicity with one another –
like the cogs, gears, and the settings of a clock.

People like things that reoccur,
because it gives them something to look forward to –
that is why people like traditions...
life is about things that are built to last,
as well as about things that happen, are captured,
and then are gone again in a snap!
Life and people will always be a work in progress
and always in the process
of constant transition.

Self-reflection

My life has always been one
of constant reinvention...
every day the man in the mirror reminds me
that you cannot move forwards
if you continue to live your life in reflection...
my life has always been one of questions,
answers, and the pursuit of mystery...
every day the voice within me
tells me to never give up, to stay true to myself,
and no matter what I do continue to be a poet
and an author of my own poetry.

We can only live our lives
by embracing what feels right at the time...
we can only see what we capture with our eyes...
we can sometimes only be free
when we are sleeping and dreaming at night...
we can only compare two sides
when we are given a deeper insight.

Some people will never truly know you,
nor ever understand why you do what you do
and sometimes that can be frustrating –
especially when you want someone to "get you",
to like you, and to want to engage with you...
some people can be drawn to people,
some people can be intimidated by people,
some people can be intrigued by people,
some people can know people
as soon as they meet them,
because they see themselves in them
as if they were their own reflection.

My Muses

It all started with my first –
the one who inspired the first poem I ever wrote;
and then, over the years, there have been
others whose names now sometimes
get stuck in my head as well as in my throat.

It has always been hard for me to move on –
to resign myself to the fact that
my relationship with some things
and with some people
has now been and is now gone.

Whenever I meet someone new
I never anticipate ever saying goodbye...
whenever I know that it might be the last time
that I get to see someone who I love
I always feel sad and I always want to cry.

If someone has inspired me
that means that there is something
profoundly special about that person...
if I have fallen for someone that means
that I made a connection with them
that for me can never be undone.

If things were once good between
someone else and I
then that must mean
that there must have been something
wonderful between us at one time –
especially at the beginning...

even when some things ultimately go bad
that does not mean that everything
that happened should make you feel
as if you wasted your time –
because what you went through
was unbelievably memorable
and deeply meaningful and inspiring.

Even after a heart breaks love lingers on...
even after you lose someone
the memories that you shared with them
continue to mean something to you –
sometimes long after you
thought them to be lost.

Your first is never your last...
you can never hide from your past...
we all have our own individual version
of a story that only we can tell our side of...
we all know what we must sacrifice
when we find someone who we instantly love.

I have loved... I have lost... I have been inspired...
I have felt fulfilled... I have felt the pain of lies...
I have felt the most powerful force known to man –
love – in times of utter darkness
that has given me hope, happiness, and light –
and it is to those people who
inspired me, once upon a time,
that I wish to pay tribute to:
those people who gave me a gift
that I will never forget
and who to me
will always be a muse.

The Environment of Nature

There is no greater aroma than
what you inhale when you
walk through a forest of trees...
there is no more heavenly experience
than witnessing and being caught in
the energy stream of the morning sunlight at dawn...
there is no place like being on a beach
while looking out to the horizon
as the sun sets below the waves...
there is no more invigorating sound
than the chorus of birdsong
that heralds both the beginning
and the end of every day...
there is no more awe-inspiring sight
than seeing planet Earth glow like a pearl
as it spins against the darkness of space...
there is no more humbling experience
than looking down at all the life
and the light that thrives and shines below
as our world silently turns on its axis
and is orbited by its own celestial offspring, The Moon...
there is no more ethereal wonder
to witness than the beautiful rippling energy strands
of the auroras of both the Northern and Southern hemispheres
created when The Sun physically reaches out
touches the thin translucent veil
of our world's atmosphere...
there is no more perfect moment
than looking up at the stars from the ground,
seeing the constellations,
seeing other planets within our solar system,
and realizing that everything and everyone
in the universe is connected.

There is so much more to life
on Earth and in the cosmos
that we have yet to discover...
there is so much more to a place
and a time than can ever be captured
or ever truly imagined...
there is so much more that humanity
can achieve together if only they
were able to put aside their differences
and talk to each other...
there is so much to be found
when you start wandering and wondering
about the greatest gift in existence:
the magical oasis of life that is
the environment of nature.

The Man at the Window

The man at the window
looks out at the world...
the man at the window doesn't move,
nor does he say a word...
the man at the window
thinks about the present
and reflects upon the past...
the man at the window
remembers a time when things
and people moved slower
and wonders why nowadays
things must fly past so fast...
the man at the window
observes life in all its infinite forms...
the man at the window
thinks about his family alive and deceased
every night when he watches the sunset
and every morning when he watches the dawn...
the man at the window
has done so many things over his life,
but now he would much rather rest...
the man at the window
has been there for countless people
and no matter what he has always done his best...
the man at the window is not being nosey –
the man at the window is taking his time
to breathe in the light of the day and to daydream...
the man at the window keeps watch
over the comings and the goings of his street –
whether that is the airplanes that fly in the sky above
or the cars that drive by on the road below...
yes, there is a special person
watching the world and continuing to stay hopeful –
and they are the man at the window.

Under the Rainbow

As soon as I saw the rainbow
I could not take my eyes off it...
as soon as I saw the multi-colored
half-circle arch across the sky
I smiled because of it...
as soon as I saw the faint spectrum
being created and projected by The Sun's light
I was in awe of it...
as soon as I saw the entrancing natural phenomena
and symbol of universal love
I immediately wondered not
what I might find at the end of it –
like some kind of magical pot of gold –
but rather what might happen
if I were instead to walk underneath it?
So, that is what I decided to do.
And what did I find when I walked
under the arc of the rainbow?
The road before me, the future,
the undiscovered opportunities
and the gifts of inspiration that await me.

Rainbows always capture the attention
and ignite the imagination of the young and the old –
but what I have discovered over my life
is that some things we find and then we lose.
Some people make promises
that they say they will keep forever
but one day they do indeed let go,
and some things entrance us for a short time
but then disappear from view.

Life is unexpected,
at the same time
that it is predictable...
life can be ugly, scary –
but life can also be beautiful...
life and light are what I see
whenever I look up at the stars at night
that though they might have
long since stopped burning
continue to shine and to glow...
life is what awaits us all
when we see
and get the opportunity
to walk under a rainbow.

Celestially Lit

Last night the tail of a meteorite
streaked across the sky...
last night a star fell to Earth
and as it burnt up in the atmosphere
those who were lucky to be looking up
were hypnotized by the sight
of this interstellar visitor being
transformed from a space rock
into a fireball of energy and light.

Whenever a piece of the cosmos
gets so close to our world
that it can almost touch it
there is always something magical about it...
whenever our ancestors witnessed
an interstellar phenomenon
they always found a way to
somehow make a record of it –
because it was always believed
that whenever a piece of outer space
was seen by the people of our planet
it was a sign and potentially heralding
a time of great change was due to begin.

Today I could feel that something
had indeed changed...
today I could feel that something –
call it a wave of fate –
was carrying me to somewhere
I needed to be once again...

today I could feel this pull –
like the force of gravity –
take me away and remind me
of who I used to be once upon a time
and who I will always be no matter
where I am or who I am with...
today was beautiful, amazing,
and transformative in so many ways...
today was full of life, nature,
and bright sunshine that shone down from above
and made sure that everything that I saw
and everywhere that I went
my eyes were gifted by the beauty
of our world that can only be seen
when nature is spectacularly
and celestially lit.

Adopt a word

Many years ago, I adopted a word –
a word that would come to define me,
a word that would come to inspire me,
a word that would come to mean
more to me than any other word –
because as soon as I saw that word
I knew who and what I was,
because I knew that that word
was me and had always been me.

Over the years I have used many words
to describe what I have seen, what I have felt,
what I believe, what people have meant
and continue to mean to me –
but there will only ever be one word
that says more than I ever could
about what it means to be someone like me:
a dreamer, a storyteller, a writer –
but not like any other,
because the word that I found
and which found me
I have come to realize has a power of its own
that can open doorways to places,
that can bring back memories of the past,
as well as give the gift of a vision
of as-yet unrealized brand-new worlds.

Many people have read what I have written,
and when I am writing from the heart
then what I write in every way is all me
and my life, as told through my poetry...
Many languages are spoken,
many languages are there to be read,
many people are constantly looking
for a purpose to their life
and for the reason why they are alive –
and from the moment that I started down
my path through life and I started to
see beauty in every facet of the world,
I knew that when I chose the word "Poet"
I had adopted a word that was in every way
who I was and who I would always be.

All in

No matter what I do, no matter who I meet,
I jump into everything with all my heart and with both feet...
I have always believed that sometimes
you need to either go all in, or go home –
because life needs to be lived
not waited for like a phone call.
No matter what has happened,
no matter what I have done,
I have lived a life of laughter and fun,
with some people who might
never again look my way and may even choose to cross
a busy street just so they do not run into me.
I have walked, I have run, I have flown, and I have fallen –
but no matter what life has thrown at me,
and no matter what people have put me through,
if my time on Earth were to end tonight
then I could honestly say that I have had a ball.
No matter the smiles, no matter the tears,
no matter the denials, no matter the fears –
I hope people who have danced with me
will remember forever where and when
we had our moments to shine in our own spotlight,
and remember that there were times
when everything felt like a dream,
because our shared moments
were better than we could have imagined.
Everybody who gives something of themselves
knows that they will never receive
in return anything close to the energy
and the love that they once gave to someone else –
but sometimes in life you must gamble,
you must show that you do not flinch,
and you must show the hand
of cards that you have been dealt and go all in.

The Talisman

Something to remind you
of somebody far away –
a loved one, a friend,
someone who you think about every day...
something as simple as an object
that somebody gave you for safe keeping
and, also, to remember them by...
something personal –
like a watch passed down and worn on the wrist
of generations of ancestors and their descendants –
that symbolizes a way back through time...
something like a mantra that is repeated
to open a door
inwards and outwards...
something like a candle that we use
when the power goes out
and we have to use the only precious light
that we have to see the path before us...
something like a photograph
taken when visiting somewhere
indescribable and meaningful
with someone who is a daily hand to hold
and a guide back to solid ground
when we find ourselves far from land...
something that gives us a feeling
of hope, optimism, as well as
a forward momentum –
because to us they will always be
a talisman.

Proof

Some people can believe in
that which they cannot see...
some people can pretend to be
someone they know that they are not...
some people need something
and someone to believe in...
some people need someone
to believe in them so that they
do not feel lost...
some people can be what for so long
they used to believe they were incapable of being...
some people go where they always
believed they would always be unwelcome...
some people have gifts with which
they can live out their dreams –
like someone with a voice who believes
that they were always born to sing...
some people want some things –
and then something happens
and all the puzzles pieces of their life
get tossed up in the air
and they must rely on the power
that sustains all who never stop believing...
some people sometimes have an experience
that is so extraordinary they
find it impossible to find the words
to make people believe what happened to them...
some people sometimes feel that they
have something to share so deeply
that they honestly believe they have to
tell the world about it by shouting
about it from their roof.

Some people want
to live a life
of love and belonging
and would do anything
and believe anyone
to have a relationship with someone
that daily deepens...
some people can naturally
accept things they receive and
"not look a gift horse in the mouth " –
whereas some people
need more of a reason
to make a change, or to make move,
because before some people
will believe something,
or the words of someone,
they sometimes need
that which is sometimes intangible:
proof.

Golden

The golden light of the sun setting
shone through my bedroom window,
as I sat thinking about time,
about my life, about the world, about the universe,
and the fact that I am truly blessed
by what I have and what I treasure
more than I could every say...
the blinding light of The Sun
that fills my eyes with glorious sunshine
inspires my thoughts and enlightens my soul
and makes me think about what
and who makes me happy every day...
the stream of sunlight that I am graced with
showers me with a purpose
and makes me smile, sigh,
and feel like a child again...
the light of the world that I see is exquisite
and the mysteries of the multiverse
that I think about as I feel myself
being carried away as if by the tide
of some interstellar ocean of energy
take away any feelings of regret and pain.
The Sun will always be there for you,
as the sun had always been there for me –
like the personification of a shepherd
that guides their flock to where they need to be –
at the same time communicating
with light what can never be told.
The glow of daylight,
as it transitions into twilight,
is bright, clear, breathtaking
and shows just how much of life
and everything that we are all bound to
is made up of a spirit that is truly golden.

Under your skin

When someone or something
gets under your skin
it can sometimes be hard
to rid yourself of them...
when someone or something
changes something fundamental about you
it can sometimes be hard
to wipe them clean from your mind...
when you lose someone or something
that gave you the gift of something amazing
when you first met them, it can be hard
to try and erase them from your life...
when someone or something
influences you like a drug
it can be hard to detoxify...
when someone or something
fills your heart with love
it can be hard to deny what to you
feels so true it could not be a lie...
when someone or something
leaves their mark upon you
it can be even more indelible than a tattoo
and too deep to ever be seen...
when someone or something
makes you feel better about yourself
than you have felt in your entire life
then you know that though they
may no longer be around physically
who and what they meant to you
will always remain with you
under your skin.

New Car Smell

There is always something
exciting about the prospect of ordering,
waiting, and then eventually getting
something you want and have been
looking forward to having in your possession...
there is always a rush of blood to the head
filled with the intoxicating cocktail
of both dopamine and adrenaline
that brings a smile to your face
whenever you have something in your grasp
that you wholeheartedly believe makes all the hard work to do
to get what you want more than worth it...
there is always a feeling of satisfaction
that bubbles up inside of you
when you are given the keys to something
and you know exactly what they symbolize
and what it is that they mean...
there is always a moment of happiness
when you take the steps down a path
that you know with utter certainty
what lies at the end and where it leads...
there is always a way to do something
that is different from how others have done it before
that may seem unconventional to some
but which rings true to you
as distinctively as that of the sound of a bell...
there is always something in the air
that you can sense rising all around you
whenever you find yourself in the driving seat
of a vehicle of opportunity that immediately
makes you feel at home, comfortable,
hopeful, and as invigorated as whenever
someone first inhales the distinctive
and intoxicating aroma of a "New Car Smell".

Open to Interpretation

When a writer writes something,
that is just the beginning...
after a writer shares what they have written
and takes it beyond the limits of their own eyes,
that is when things truly get exciting...
when a writer first gets an idea they never truly know
what it will ultimately come to be...
when a writer uses their gift
and naturally infuses a part of themselves
into whatever they have written or are writing
they always leave something
that they may not have planned for their readers to read.
When a writer lets their words go
they can have no idea by whom, when,
nor where their art will be enjoyed –
and there is no knowing why, nor how,
their words will touch a reader
and inspire their dreams as they lie asleep in bed...
when a writer first puts pen to paper,
or finger to key, they must resist
any and every thought that might occur to them
in which they might attempt to cross out,
erase, or delete something of them that they felt had to be said.
When a writer creates something
of their own heart, mind, soul, and imagination
there is always an exchange of energy
that takes place that can cross
time and distance instantly...
even if the first intention of a writer
after a while becomes like that of a whisper,
the first spark of inspiration that brought an idea to life
will always be there to be felt, read, heard, seen,
and like the world of a dream
open to interpretation.

Taken

Over the years I have taken people
on a journey with me...
over the years I have literally held
the hand of people and guided them
to places and to things that are important to me...
over the years I have told people things
that only they would know about me...
over the years I have opened the mind
of people to what is impossible,
and I too have been fascinated
by what happens when there is
a coming together of many feelings,
emotions, colours, and expressions
of what makes a difference to the way
that people live, love, think, and believe.

Over the years I have always been someone
who goes that extra mile...
over the years I have always been someone
who would rather leave a lasting impression
in the form of a smile...
over the years I have always been someone
who would spend time doing something
that I knew in the long run would be worthwhile...
over the years I have always been someone
who knew that there was always more
to be known about the substance
of something or someone
rather than their style.

Over the years I have felt drawn
to things, to places, to people,
from the moment that I have awoken...
over the years I have felt as if
I am only able to keep ahold
of some things for a short amount of time
before they are forsaken...
over the years I have felt found,
abandoned, made whole, and then broken...
over the years I have felt, and I have seen,
change happen right in front of me,
I have experienced the arrival
of hope and joy before my eyes,
I have made the most of every moment
that I have been given
and I always try to return the favour
of whatever or whomever I meet
wherever I find myself being taken.

Feel

I will never change...
I will forever be the same...
my heart is my heart, my face is my face...
I have felt soaked through to the bone
by the fallen raindrops of the rain...
I have felt burned as if by a fire's infinite flames...
I have felt pain as if I have been
shot in chest by a gun...
I have felt inspiration like a lightbulb
literally turned on in my brain
and showed me things that used to be hidden...
I have felt exhilaration like the g-force
that pins a fighter pilot
in the ejector-seat of their cockpit.
I have felt the tender touch of a child...
I have felt the powerful kiss of a lover...
I have felt the happiness of a true smile...
I have felt myself be pulled up and over...
I have felt the sadness of being forgotten…
I have felt more alive than ever
whenever someone has told me
that to them I am important.
I have felt the world stop...
I have felt time disappear in a flash...
I have felt alone and lost.
I have felt the present eclipse the past...
I have felt so many instances of hope come to me
as if they were a film being projected in my imagination
through the lens of my dreams that always allow me to see
what was, what is, and what could be.
I have felt things that have reinvigorated me
that are unquestionably the real deal...
I have felt things that I wish
everybody could feel.

The Crow

When I walked out of my house this morning
I immediately found myself
staring into the dark eyes of a crow –
it was as if the crow knew something
about me and about what was going
to happen to me that I did not know.
I stared at the crow, as they stared back at me,
and then when I started walking towards
them they let me get perhaps two feet
before they decided to flap their wings
and take flight as quietly, as quickly,
and as effortlessly as could be.
I didn't think anything else of the crow –
until just now, as a matter of fact:
as I wonder how long it will take
before I once again feel whole again,
and just like the old me;
however, I know that it is too late
for some things and that there are some things
that will forever remain in the past.
We are all a product of the choices that we have made
and the road that we walk upon
that is built upon our hopes, our dreams,
as well as our fears and our actions
that we cannot take back.

When I woke up this morning
I knew that something was waiting for me –
something that I knew would leave a scar
upon me that only I will wear
and that only I would know...
when I woke up this morning
I was given a message
meant only for me
that when I think about it now
was as clear as clear could be –
and the messenger of this message
was who was waiting for me
outside my house this morning:
none other than the black bird
that is smarter than you could know,
and symbolically considered to be
the herald of change, transition,
transformation and new beginnings
that is The Crow.

Solaris

A blue sky above your head...
The Sun shining brightly...
a day at the beach with friends...
walking through a park
while enjoying the sights and the sounds
all around that resonate with natural beauty...
a smile, a laugh, a series of newly made memories...
a song, a vibe, something that leaves
an impression of itself with you...
a roller-coaster at a funfair that sees
you go up, down, and sideways...
a ceremony of matrimony that reminds
everybody who witnesses it
that a certain combination of souls are meant
to be bound together like glue...
a family get-together...
an event you do not want to miss...
a trip to somewhere that you swear
you will remember forever –
there are some things that feel perfect
and feel meant to be because of the touch,
the light and the energy that is captured
from The Sun and made a part of us
that we would never want to miss.

Games

It always amazes me
what draws people together...
it always astounds me
what people will do to feel something...
it always surprises me
what can be seen and what can be heard
when people become observers
as well as participants of a communal experience
of excitement and wonder...
it always fascinates me
what people are willing to do
when they are given the freedom
and the gift to be anything
and to say anything they want.

For centuries, crowds and audience members
have stood, sat, cheered, and clapped
while watching fighters in a fight,
competitors in a competition,
players in a game face-off against one another...
for all of time, there has been a race
between multiple sides in which
the object is to dominate and be the victor...
whenever there is a contest to out-do,
to out-play, and to overshadow someone else
there is always a start and a finish,
there are always winners
and there are always losers,
and sometimes when people bring their "A game"
they can even surprise themselves
with just how good they can be
when they put their all into that which they love...

whenever a particular moment arrives
for someone to shine like they have been
preparing to do for hours, for days,
for months, perhaps even for years,
players, athletes, thrill-seekers all
always find the strength, the speed,
the spirit, the will, the heart
to go as far as they can possibly go,
like a rocket ship to the heavens above.

It can feel life-changing to be somewhere
with a multitude of people
at a once in a lifetime opportunity
to witness something phenomenal,
fulfilling, and magical...
it can be engrossing to feel as if
you are a part of something bigger
than you believe you are,
but at the same time something you feel
inextricably a part of –
as if you are staring at a piece of art in a gallery
and you feel like you can step inside the frame...
it can be entertaining, electrifying,
enlightening, enlivening, enriching
to be pulled into something that
while you are doing it looks,
and most likely feels,
wonderful and enjoyable...
it can be hard to resist picking a team,
picking a side, picking a sport,
picking something to engage your attention in –
like one of the many encompassing
games of the world.

What we leave behind

Every day we all meet people
who influence our thoughts,
our feelings, our emotions, our actions,
our intentions going forward –
what keeps us awake during the day
and what keeps us dreaming at night...
every day I see, and I experience,
a wave of connection touch me –
sometimes slow, gentle, and subtle,
sometimes fast, hard, and heavy –
and sometimes I know immediately
what this force that I feel means to me;
but sometimes it takes some time
for me to realize what has impacted upon me
and upon what path it will ultimately lead me.

Every day we all give others gifts
that might be big, that might be small,
that might be useful, that might be short-lived,
that might be indelible like a tattoo,
that might be beautiful like a genuine smile
that makes a person's face beam
brighter than the brightest sunlight...
every day I share what has inspired me,
what has got under my skin,
what has changed me,
what shows itself from below the surface
of my consciousness ocean
like a shark's dorsal fin.

Every day we all leave an impression on people,
just like someone's footsteps do upon the wet sand
of a beach when the tide goes in and out,
and sometimes the impressions left
last longer than they were expected to...
every day I am grateful for certain things,
I am grateful for certain people,
I am grateful for certain choices that I have made,
I am grateful for certain experiences,
certain moments in time,
and certainties of life...
every day we all interact with objects
that have been on a journey
from the moment of their creation –
like a message in a bottle
that finds itself bobbing up and down
and being carried far across the sea,
or like a pair of shoes that take
their wearer miles before it is time
for them to give up the ghost.

Every day I hope that I have had
a positive influence and I have made
positive impacts upon everybody I have met –
whether in person, literally,
virtually, intentionally, or indirectly –
and that people who might be old friends,
new friends, strangers, and those
who know me by my face and my name,
but not yet personally,
are grateful and they will always be thankful
for whatever it is of mine that they find
which I have left behind.

Breaking Habits

Like the needle of a record player
when a vinyl album reaches its conclusion,
in life people can feel like they have been
thrown out of a groove that they have been in
when they reach the ultimate end
of a particular cycle or revolution...
it can be jarring; it can be hard to find your place again...
it can be worrying; it can be like finding yourself
driving down a highway and then drifting
out of your lane.

Over time everybody naturally picks up habits
that come to define them and sustain them...
over time everybody exhibits new attitudes
and new mannerisms that are noticeable
to every observer of human behavior...
over time everybody starts doing things
that they probably should not do
because they are motivated more
by what their heart,
rather than what their head,
is telling them...
over time everybody does things
that might feel like déjà vu moments
of similar instances
that might have happened before.

Over time old myths always become replaced
by new myths with new names and new faces...
things we used to do, and people we used to see
and interact with every day,
over time become replaced
by new things, and by new people
who we become familiar with.

What and who people think are bad for us
is always open to interpretation,
and sometimes it can take some time
to realize that like a bottle of pop
a relationship has lost its fizz...
we are all habitual by nature –
from our psychology to our biology –
which is why it is not surprising
that we do the same things repeatedly.
But, sometimes, for your own good,
you must do something
that might once have felt impossible:
you must stop doing
some things you have been doing
and you must change the life
that you have been living
by breaking some of your
most definable
good and bad habits.

The Baton

It is only natural for things to continuously
be passed from one person to another,
from one place to another, from one time to another –
because life is an endless continuum of infinite connections.
Thoughts, feelings, emotions, experiences,
scenarios always find a way to reoccur, repeat,
and be revived for another setting,
for another generation –
but the key part of what makes them
so everlasting always remains intact.
Depending on how life is lived
informs how echoes of the past
will be interpreted by the present,
as well as by the future...
trends, fashions, attitudes,
buried treasure, lost keepsakes
have a way of returning to the surface
from wherever they found themselves
until the time was right for them
to be found once again.
People see perfection in nature...
people see perfection in art...
people hear perfection
in the way that someone laughs...
people see perfection in patterns...
some people see perfection in math.
Everybody finds something in their life
that instantly takes away their fear
and makes the path before them clear...
like people participating in a race,
or a collective journey of togetherness,
everybody is constantly picking up,
passing on, and re-enlivening
life's universal and constantly moving baton.

The English Summer

The Summer sun has arrived upon the shores,
on the beaches, on the hills, in the parks, in the gardens,
and on the streets of the cities of our island country...
the Summer sun has bestowed
upon the flowers, the trees,
the animals, the insects, the birds,
the people of the place I call home
a fresh wave of warmth and connection
like the tides of an ever-present ocean...
the Summer sun has people breaking out their barbecues
and gathering to feast with one another...
the Summer sun has people coming out of their shell
to sing, to dance, and to revel with each other...
the Summer sun has people
freeing themselves of their inhibitions...
the Summer sun has people
feeling like the time is right to
to go to places of beauty and fascination...
the Summer sun has a draw to it
that is the perfect stage for nature
to display its kaleidoscope of infinite colours...
the Summer sun has the gift
to be able to rejuvenate the spirit
and the gift to be able to give
an insight into the human experience –
but the Summer sun is also
something to enjoy in small doses,
because too much may cause more harm than good.
The Summer sun is shining bright in the sky,
and as I bask in its rays, I feel something
that reminds me of something I have felt, and I know well:
the odyssey of emotions and feelings
that all come together at the height
of the English Summer.

Interesting Times

Some people want to live a life
that is undemanding, easy, quiet, and hassle-free...
some people want to live a life living and doing
the same things every day...
some people sometimes make a wish that their life
was more thrilling and fuller of experiences and events
that might add more depth and colour to a seemingly
black and white existence...
some people sometimes believe that if they meet the right person
then their entire life would make sense
and they would feel complete.
Some people want things
that they cannot have, should not have,
but they want them anyway...
some people say they want the truth –
but, in the end, they find out
that they might have been happier believing a lie.
Some people have this instinct to reach for the highest point,
to stand upon the highest summit,
to go fast and to not think about
who and what they might encounter along their journey...
some people can seemingly do nothing
and for some reason someone will not like them.
Some people like rollercoasters and slides...
some people like the challenge of a climb...
some people sometimes find themselves
living in a maelstrom of their own choices, actions,
and emotions that makes them
pine for when the weather around them
was more predictable, pleasant, and fine...
some people do things in their life
and there comes a moment when they realize
the true meaning of the wish/curse
"May you live in interesting times".

Screen Heroes

When I was a child,
whenever I watched someone
doing something in a TV show or a movie
I always immediately began to imagine
myself as if I were who I saw
and I wanted to be them in real life...
I remember watching Kevin Costner
as Robin Hood and immediately afterwards
wanting to pick up a bow and arrow,
to live in Sherwood Forest,
and to be just like the *"Prince of Thieves"*...
I remember watching "Star Wars"
when Obi-wan Kenobi is telling
Mark Hamill's Luke Skywalker that
"The Force will be with him"
and hoping that throughout my life
The Force would also be with me...
I remember watching Harrison Ford
as Indiana Jones and afterwards
feeling drawn to becoming
an archaeologist who uncovered and revealed
the stories and the mysteries of history...
I remember watching Marty McFly
traveling in the DeLorean time machine
and leaving a fiery trail after it reached 88mph
and wanting to be a time traveler just like him
and go *"Back to the Future"*...
I remember watching William Shatner
as Captain James T. Kirk travelling
at warp speed on the starship Enterprise
in "Star Trek" and wanting to also take a voyage
to the final frontier and across the galaxy...

I remember seeing Christopher Reeve
as Superman and immediately believing
that it was possible for a man to fly...
I remember watching multiple actors
play James Bond and wanting to be
by their side as they drove at full speed
in their Aston Martin through the streets
of some exciting and interesting city...
I remember being a child
and being a captivated, enthralled,
motivated, inspired, at the same time
hearing the call to adventure
and wish fulfillment
by so many of my life-long
screen heroes.

Parting Ways

It can be easy;
if can be hard...
you can feel free;
you can feel lost –
but there comes a time when
one must become two again,
because that is the way
things are meant to be.
Things, people, can start out
and seem disparate and different from one another –
but, over time, when multiple
elements are mixed,
a new state of equanimity can be created and there is
perfect harmony, maybe even a love.
However, most things are not meant
to last forever – even though
you may desperately want them to –
and gradually tensions and tears
start appearing it what was once
a seemingly perfect relationship,
and then things can get too bad
and they become too far gone to fix
and what follows is the eventual end of things.
No one ever wants to envision
the last time they do something...
no one ever wants to consider
what might happen when something stops...
"goodbye" is a word no one wants to say –
but things happen, things change,
people change, people grow apart,
and sometimes you have to do something
as devastating and heartbreaking
as walking away and partings ways.

Vibes

It can happen instantly; it can happen in a flash...
it can flow easily like water,
or like the words of poetry...
it can happen fast.

They can be like a faint rumble; they can be like a tsunami...
they can make you feel humble, they can make you feel free.

It can start as simply as hearing a song playing on the radio...
it can begin with something as perfect as a smile...
it can last longer than something that can be seen or shown...
it can find you at the same time
as you find them and as regularly
as the shadow of a sundial.

They can be bad... they can be good...
they can be sad... they can be misunderstood.
However, whenever anybody
finds themselves somewhere,
sometime, perhaps with someone
who also feels what they feel,
and on the same frequency
it can be more powerful than
the gravity of the Moon that creates
the ocean's infinite tides.
There is no way of mistaking
the sensations, the emotions, the feeling of elation,
the tingle of electricity that accompanies
the rise of the spirit within
that can inspire the thoughts,
that can move the body,
that can overcome and compel anyone
with a wave of multi-layered
and meaningful vibes.

Arise

Like a wave of solar energy,
the solstice and the longest day
heralded the arrival of not only new light,
but also of new hope, of new optimism,
and a new reason to live,
and a new reason to love, as well...
like a soft breeze through a field of daisies,
the sight of nature all around us
reminds all who want to see it
the unbreakable connection
that exists between all things
that is so innocent, so important,
so serene, so peaceful, so beautiful...
like a dream made real,
wherever people get the opportunity
to embrace the gift of what nature is –
like when someone sets foot upon
the wet sand of a beach
or they go for a paddle
in the shallows of the sea,
or like in 1966 when Neil Armstrong
set foot on the Moon –
there is always this impact
and this imprint made
that reverberates
like a guitar string
or like the skin of a drum...

like a drop of water on a desert floor,
like a tap on a windowpane
by the beak of a bird,
like the moment a child
first sees their reflection,
like the moments when you feel as if
time has stood still for you for some reason,
or like watching a butterfly flutter their wings –
there is so much detail, depth,
meaning, and spirit to feel,
to breathe in, to embrace,
and to make a part of you,
from which there is no
knowing what will follow;
but sometimes you must
let things arise naturally -
like the spark of love, life, light
that can be seen in a person's eyes.

Poetry is My Religion

Whenever I open my eyes,
whenever I close my eyes,
within me, around me,
I know that I am not alone...
whenever I am confronted by
the spectre of fear and doubt
I know that I can instantly connect
with a wellspring of hope...
whenever I feel like I do not know
what to do or where to go
I know that I am on a path
of enlightenment that I started upon
from the day that I was born...
whenever I find myself thinking,
feeling, dreaming, allowed
to let my mind, my heart, my spirit
and my soul wander I always hear
the voice of the eternal call...
whenever I can, wherever I am –
whether sitting on a bench in a park,
whether sitting at a table in a cafe,
whether in my bedroom looking out the window,
I feel connected to the world, to the universe,
to nature, to the sun of the day
and to the stars of the night sky,
and I also feel connected to people
from my past life, from my present life,
and perhaps to those who I have yet to meet
who I do not yet know I am connected to,
and who do not yet know are already connected to me.

Whenever I have sought out
the next signpost that will lead me
to what direction I am destined to take
down the multitude of roads
of choice and fate I know that
whether I am surrounded by tall trees,
by tall buildings, by nature, or by people,
I am free to be and to free to experience
what and with whom I am supposed to
my own personal perception of life
and follow my faith of hope and optimism
that lies at the heart of what I believe,
what I live by, and what speaks to me
and every day convinces me
that poetry in all its forms
is my religion.

The Switch

When I first began writing poetry
it was like a light had been switch on...
when I first began writing poetry
it was at the same time that I fell in love...
when I first began writing poetry
it was like walking outdoors
and feeling the touch of the sun...
when I first began writing poetry
it was like I already knew that I was
a poet for life and not just for the moment.

Some things you think you
know for sure and forever –
but then they change...
some people you think you know
as well as you know your own face –
but then they take a hard left
down an unexpected alley...
some things look perfect
with the right lighting –
but their flaws become apparent
when seen in the light of day...
some people look idealistic from far away –
but up-close everybody's cracks are exposed
like the shadows of monuments in a valley.

I did not know what was inside of me
until I found the right person
with the right key to unlock
the door of my library of internal poetry...
I did not know what would happen
after I started walking down this road
that I have been on now for years –

but I knew that would never be truly alone
and that there would always be
something and someone with me...
I did not know what it meant
to have been found until I felt my eyes,
my mind, my heart, my ears, my soul
open wide and never want
to miss a thing about anything
and everything ever again...
I did not know what lay beyond the horizon,
in outer space, or in the dark,
until I saw that there is always
a way and a gift for me to turn to
and to turn on whenever I want to
like a switch.

The Romantic

I have always been a romantic...
I have always loved caring
for someone and showing them affection...
I have always understood the power
and the depth of the words of poetry,
even before I knew that I too
had a heart and soul that was poetic...
I have always felt blessed
whenever I have been somewhere
with someone who I could look at
all day with spellbinding fascination.

I have always been able to look
at people and see what was inside of them...
I have always been able to hear the call
of someone's internal voice loud and clear...
I have always been able to see things
and situations through a multi-layered,
multi-textured and multi-coloured lens...
I have always been able to sit silently
and hear only the sound of my own
heart beating in my chest
and not once feel any kind of fear.

I have always been someone
who could wax lyrical about
what a single red rose can teach us
about people and about ourselves...
I have always been someone who appreciates
the power and the importance of ceremony,
traditions, keeping things
as they are for as long as they can,
because I am innately nostalgic...

I have always been someone
who knew that doing what you love,
with whom you love, is always
going to be good for your health...
I have always been someone
who loves meeting new people,
finding out who they are
and what their hidden story is –
because I have always believed
that there is a power of the universe
that can only be known and wielded
by those who are openly romantic.

Jubilee

It is always good to have
a moment of celebration...
it is always rejuvenating to have
a time of reconciliation...
it is always amazing to have
a gathering together of people
at a special event or a party...
it is always wonderful to see
an entire nation of people young and old
seemingly united, excited,
and proud to be who and what they are,
as they take the time to display
and wave the flag of their home,
while also recognizing the achievement
of longevity and leadership of their
Head of State, their Monarch,
at the time of a milestone jubilee.

There is a reason why children and adults
love watching fireworks explode at night...
there is a reason why people
love going to places and doing things
they do not do every day...
there is a reason why children and adults
love the escapism of books, films, television,
radio, music, streaming, games,
and why some people actively go looking for
a reason to physically jump after a fright...
there is a reason why some people
like to get dressed up and make even more
of an effort than they usually do,
and it is usually to signify the importance
to them of a special date.

Everybody needs hope in their life...
everybody needs something and someone
to look to and to believe in...
everybody needs to fulfil a dream...
everybody needs light...
everybody occasionally needs a win...
everybody sometimes needs to be
around as many people of their kin,
their country, or their kingdom,
at a moment of feverish,
collective, jubilation.

Before Breakfast

Every morning, for as long as I can remember,
I have been waking up
with a head full of ideas –
often inspired by dreams that I
might have had the night before,
or recollections of things that might
have happened –
and, as a result, I always find myself
sitting up in bed, standing up on my feet,
thinking in between blinking,
as well as allowing my mind to wander
until it settles upon somewhere,
upon someone, or upon something
who drives my thoughts even further
down the road I find myself on.

Every morning, for as long as I can remember,
I have been waking up early
and then reaching out to the rest of the world,
catching up on the conversations of the moment,
as well as immersing myself in
the important and the superficial
things that I see which I know
mean something to somebody,
but not always as much to me.

Every morning, for as long as I can remember,
I have been waking up to the music
that always helps me to find
the right groove to start my day off with –
like dropping the needle of a record player
onto a vinyl disc and immediately finding
the start of a favourite song
on a particular album.

Every morning,
for as long as I can remember,
I have been waking up
with a head full of poetry...
every morning,
for as long as I can remember,
I have had these intuitive feelings
about what might happen
in the short-term future,
as well as flashbacks to the past.

Every morning,
for as long as I can remember,
I have found myself posing questions,
finding answers, and wondering about possibilities –
all the while knowing that there is
more to life to discover than what I
or anyone thinks they might know –
and all this every morning,
and usually before breakfast.

Maverick

I have never minded flying solo...
I have never minded going my own way
rather than going with the flow...
I have never minded thinking
differently than those around me...
I have never minded being independent
because having the gift of independence
is the key to being free.

Even as a boy I knew that my path
through life would be different
from that of my friends...
as a child, and still now, I was never afraid
to take a leap into the unknown
while those around me stand still and stare,
as I choose to push down on the throttle
and go to where others might not dare.

I have always enjoyed the thrill
and the adrenaline rush
of going against conformity...
I have always loved running
and being fast on my feet...
I have always wanted to push the envelope
and be catapulted to the outer reaches
of time, possibility, and space...
I have always wanted to be, and I always will be,
whether inside or outside a cockpit,
a test pilot, a rebel, a rocket man,
a daredevil, and a maverick.

Exodus

People are leaving...
there appears to be a mass exodus...
people are choosing to uproot themselves
and start a new chapter in a new setting;
however, there are still the shadows left
of those whose presence we will never forget.
Places change, people change...
nothing and no one is
ever meant to stay the same...
photographs that start out
as symbols of hope and optimism
over time do begin to fade...
after something monumental happens
that shakes the foundations of s-omewhere
people are always left in shock
and always look around and want answers
from those who they believe are ultimately to blame.
There is always a first time for everything,
and there is always a last time...
everything and everyone wants and needs trust...
there is always a feeling of disappointment
when people realize that they have
been deceived into believing a lie.
Everyone has to make the right decisions for them
at the time that they are faced with a choice –
and, for some people, when they look around
and at their surroundings, and they think about
how, who, and what they have always known
might have changed in ways
that are unpalatable for them to remain,
they sometimes choose to make
the life-changing leap with others
who have also chosen to
undertake an exodus.

The Restless Club

I cannot sleep... I have insomnia...
for some reason, my mind
is too active to switch off,
as if it is flooded with too many thoughts,
too many feelings, too many ideas –
leaving me staring at the clock.

As I have laid here in bed,
under the covers, with my eyes momentarily closed,
and then open wide,
I have been thinking and wondering
about life and where the lights
of my journey have taken me...
I have been flicking through
the many pages of the book
of where I have been,
with whom, why, and how,
and considering the many rhyming verses
of my internal and external poetry.

I do not know why this happened
tonight of all nights –
but what I realized was that,
like everything, I was meant to be
awake for a reason...
I do not know why, what, or who
stopped me from sleeping the whole night through;
but because of not being able to sleep
I chose to do something I had
not truly done for a while: listen –
and what did I hear at this early hour?
Nothing, no one – and yet I know that
something and someone were right there with me
holding my hand and telling me not to hold back.

I know that most people would rather
be sleeping when everybody else
around them is doing the same,
but no matter what someone is doing
someone else on the other side
of the world may be doing the complete opposite –
and for every person who can
sleep all night and every night
there are those whose mind
sometimes finds it hard
to get the rest that it needs,
and though most of the time
I can and do sleep like a log
tonight, this morning, I find myself
a poetry writing member
of The Restless Club.

Honour Among Poets

Poets would not, should not,
and could not steel from one another –
however a poet may deliberately,
or perhaps unknowingly,
be inspired by another poet
to create their own work of word art.
The poetry of poets always echoes
beyond the page they are written upon –
even before there was the printing press,
the telegram, the telephone, the fax,
the Internet, email, and social media,
the inspiration of a poet spread far and wide
using word of mouth.
Poets have their own thought process,
their own writing style,
their own tried and tested truth
that they like to share that can be
as vague as a cloud or as direct as a dart.
The poems of poets may speak volumes
about whom they are and what drives them artistically,
while at the same being as short as a sonnet.
Poets wake up every day looking,
listening, and experiencing things
differently than those around them –
and sometimes poets can look at
the same something that they looked at
only the day before and see something
unique and worth remembering,
repeating, and sharing.

Poetry comes from familiarity,
as well as from uncertainty...
poetry comes from the mind,
as well as from the soul of an artist,
and the connection that they have
to a source of creation as powerful
as The Sun's rays upon a garden
that inspires all forms of life
to collect and spread nature's natural energy.

Poets are the interpreters as well
as the guides to what is ordinarily
overlooked by those who sometimes
only see the world in black and white...
poetry is the expression and the echo
of someone who has a lot to say
but who may sometimes find it hard
to express in person their thoughts,
their feelings, their experiences, and their desires –
and while some might use the poetry of others
to extend and deepen their insight into the human soul,
those who are sensitive to such things
can rest assured that there will always be
honour among poets.

Make Your Own Bed

Some things in life will
always be out of our control,
some things in life will
always be out of our reach –
but some things in life
are completely ours to do
with what we will...
some things in life will
always be a dream to aspire to
and to be inspired by…
some things in life
will always be as ephemeral
as a cloud in the sky –
but some things in life
can open both doors and windows
within us and around us that can
make us literally leap on through
to a world of something
that once seemed incredible and unobtainable.

Some things in life are just meant to happen,
some things in life are just meant to be,
some things in life are meant to have a plan –
but there are some things in life
that are a matter of "we shall see",
because every day we all interact with
a world of people and things,
of infinite complexity,
and often comforting predictability.

Some things in life we need to know everything about
and some things we can comfortably
live in the dark about and in a state of deniability...
some things in life we can leave for others to do,
and there some things in life
that we cannot say –
but there are times when we must
do some things, and there are times
when some things must be said.

Sometimes you must clean up
the mess you have made...
sometimes you must do your best
at setting things right with people –
including long lost family and friends;
but no matter what has been said,
and no matter what has been done,
if each of us realize that
though there are times when we can leave
some things and some people alone
to eventually become what and who
they are supposed to be,
there will always be a time when
every one of us have
to make our own bed because
no one else can do it for us.

The things that we will do

Sometimes it is amazing
the lengths that people will go to...
sometimes it is amazing
the things that people will do
for a friend, for a family member,
for a companion, for a stranger
to help them out
and give them support in some way...
sometimes people will do things
for the people who mean the most to them
that they would not dream of doing for anyone else;
however, when the time arrives
and when the need arises
for someone to step up
and do something extraordinary
some people always manage
to go the extra mile, to pull out all the stops,
to make sure that their devotion
for someone is in full display...
sometimes the things people will do
for love are the most extreme –
some people have been known
to act in such a manner
and to accomplish such feats of inspiration
and endurance that they might rival
those with the greatest intellectual
or physical prowess.

Sometimes the things
that people can accomplish
when the clock is ticking
and when time is running out
and when a decisive decision needs to be made
speak volumes about the capability
and the capacity of people –
especially when they are under duress...
sometimes life tests us all,
because sometimes something or someone
wants to see what we're all made of
and to what tune our heart rings true...
sometimes it amazes me what things
people, including myself,
depending on the time
and the place we find ourselves,
will ultimately be compelled to do.

First Contact

The moment of first contact is particularly important...
the moment of first contact
is when everything is still new...
the moment of every first contact
is always different...
the moment of first contact
can be when the first links of a chain
are forged together with something
stronger than glue...
the moment of first contact
can be fraught with both mystery
and sometimes confusion
until all the waves and the creases
of uncertainty have been smoothed out...
the moment of first contact
is when people first start
finding out who someone else is –
and sometimes first contact
can also turn out to be last contact...
the moment of first contact
is a lesson for all the moments to follow...
the moment of first contact
can feel like forever, or it can be forgettable –
depending upon what interests
and intentions are on a person's mind...
the moment that you first meet someone
you have never met before
you have no idea, nor control, of how things will go,
nor how things will turn out –
but what you can do is hope
for the best that whatever first contact
you have will be memorable,
in a good way, and will open the door
for more contact in the future.

One Thing Leads To Another

It always amazes me how fast
one thing can lead to another...
it always feels somehow supernatural
when one action has the unexpected
occurrence of causing a domino effect
that slowly reveals a hidden image or pattern
just waiting to be pieced together...
it always seems unbelievable whenever
I see order lead to chaos,
and whenever I saw chaos lead to order...
it always makes me smile how
a single song, a simple gesture,
or a small gift of kindness
can make a heart take flight...
it always seems somehow natural
whenever I feel drawn,
like a hummingbird to a flower,
to people who for some reason
I know immediately will
change and influence me for the better...
it is always a rush whenever I
enter, or re-enter, into something,
or into somewhere, I have not, or I have,
been before that always had to happen –
because like the seemingly random
things that somehow happen in life,
throughout the universe,
one thing will always lead to another.

Converse

I have always loved to talk...
I have always loved to meet new people...
I have always allowed my enthusiasm for life
to guide me ever since I could walk...
I have always been able to find something
to converse with someone about –
no matter how big or how small...
I have always loved discovering
what I have in common with others
and what others have in common with me...
I have always loved taking the time
to listen and to learn from people
who have no idea just how insightful
and interesting they can effortlessly be...
I have always loved the thought that we
here on Earth are constantly transmitting
and communicating the infinite layers
of what makes us who we are
out into the vast expanse of the universe...
I have always loved the idea that there
are also those out there, in every galaxy,
who every minute of every day are also
listening and sending out
their own voice and their own message –
accidentally, or deliberately, trying to
reach out and converse.

Deus Poetica

I feel like I have just awoken from a ten year-long dream...
I feel like I have just spent a decade being inspired, inspiring,
and embodying the spirit of the God of Poetry...
I feel like all the drama
that came before has been washed away...
I feel like I have stepped through a door
and out into the world of a brand-new day –
but one that does not resemble
all that have come before in any way...
I feel like I have emerged and arisen
from a shell wherein which I grew
and I matured into who and what I am now...
I feel like I can now be something
and someone I could not have been in the past...
I feel like I am now unchained...
I feel like from now on
I will not be mind-tricked by those
who see me as a means to an end.
I feel like the pieces of life's puzzle
are once again moving to create a new picture...
I feel like I am traveling towards
something that will redefine my life
and build the reality of my future...
I feel like I can take a step back,
while I take a step forward,
and at any given moment plant new roots
and at the same that I grow new leaves,
apples, and flowers upon the branches
of my ever-changing inspiration tree...
I feel like I can hear the voice of the divine
telling me that everything is going to be fine
and that one day once again I will find
the inspiration that will add to the life's work
of the eternal God of Poetry.

End of the Road

Every life has a beginning and an end...
every journey has a start and a finish...
every day has a message to be received
and a message to be sent...
every time you hope for the best
sometimes you get exactly what you wanted
and sometimes the reality that unfolds
in no way matches your original wish.

As I stand at the junction
at the end of one road
and at the beginning of another
I find myself looking back
over the path that I have forged
with my own words and actions
and I see so many of the missteps
that I have made –
as if I could see my own footprints
as clearly as if they were made
in snow or in mud –
and I wish that I were able to
go back and change certain things;
because now I realize that for so long
I have, in a way, been trying
to hold back the water of a flood
by constantly repairing breaches
in the dams that I have constructed
to not allow the natural flow
of the poetry of life that I believe in
to change and refresh that which
sometimes needs to be renewed –
because for so long I have been held back
by emotional barriers that at times
I found it hard to contend with and understand.

Everything is finite...
night must become day,
just as day must become night...
rain falls, seas rise, rivers flow –
and no matter what is said
and what is done nature will win out,
and for every door that opens
one must close...
everything, everyone,
can only be expected
to go so far for so long
before they reach
the end of a road
and they must
start upon another.

Keep Fighting

Don't give up, do your best,
keep going, keep fighting –
that is what I have been taught to do all my life
and that is what I have done...
stand up for what you believe in,
stand your ground, face your adversary,
stay calm, don't be afraid, don't run –
that is what I have tried to do
whenever I have found myself
in a David and Goliath situation
when I have found myself face to face
with something or someone more imposing.
I have never liked bullies,
and although in school I was called
names about my height and how I looked
I have never allowed the words of others
to get under my skin and make me
think that I was anything or anyone less than I was –
I always just assumed that some people
had a problem with me for reason
which was not my problem and I could not do anything
to change their mind even if I wanted to.
I am mostly a pacifist who believes
that peace, ideas and words are powerful
and are essential to change the world;
however, if given the option to have
to defend my right to exist and to preserve
my way of life and the life of others,
I would be willing to show who I am
and what I stand for:
freedom of self-expression for everyone
and the freedom to love anything or anyone –
in any way imaginable,
because I am not afraid.

When I was younger,
I was much more reserved...
when I was younger,
I mostly kept myself to myself...
when I was younger, I had friends –
but I knew that I was different from
everybody else my age,
which is a superpower I have learned...
when I was younger, I had my share
of disagreements with people young and old –
but now that I am older, I realize
that sometimes it is better to
say nothing and keep walking,
because there will come a time for everyone
when the cards of fate will be dealt...
when I was younger, I was as fast
and as full of energy as a bolt of lightning –
but now that I am older, I am sure
that I am not as fast-footed as I was in my youth;
however, I know that if ever I found myself
having to defend my home,
my family, my people, my hopes, my dreams,
then I would not hesitate to do
what must be done and do what I have
always been taught to do:
to stay hopeful and to keep fighting.

One Day

One day to return to life...
One day to walk in the sunlight once again...
One day to feel the wind upon my face...
One day to hear the music
that traverses and connects all the spheres
that dance through the blackness of space...
One day to smell the ever-present
perfume of the flowers of the world's garden...
One day to feel the sensation
of raindrops upon my skin...
One day to look in the mirror
and see the face of the person
I used to be recognized as...
One day to look through faded photos
of forgotten memories from the past...
One day to go to a beach and write my name in the sand
before it and I are once again washed away by the tide...
One day to look at a clock and wonder
why people are so obsessed with time...
One day to visit the places that I remember going to...
One day to roll a dice and find out
what fate's hand will choose...
One day to laugh... One day to cry...
One day to fall backwards
and then look up at the clouds of the sky...
one to smile and then say:
life is the gift that you don't realize
you have been given until it is taken away –
but when things end
sometimes you get a chance to revisit
the world you knew and revel in its beauty,
but when that time comes
make the most of it
because you may only get one day.

Dinosaurs had feathers

You can learn something new every day...
you may know how to do something
backwards and forwards –
but there are times when we can all be surprised,
even by something familiar,
in a new and an unexpected way...
whether you are young or old
life and people can, do, and will
always find a way to surprise you –
like a twist that often happens
within the story of a book, or a movie,
that makes you reconsider all that
you thought you knew about why
and what the storyteller, or the director,
wanted to convey or display.

Sometimes after we unearth
something that had been buried,
or after we believe we have discovered
everything about what makes something work,
someone will look at something
and find evidence that makes the world
take a second look at what they thought
was the truth of something, or someone,
and present a different version of what is,
and what was, and in an instant
can rewrite the history book version
and paint a brand-new picture
that will define perceptions and conceptions
for generations to come.

Unfortunately, to our knowledge,
no one has invented a time machine
that can be used to go back
and corroborate the physical appearance
of legendary and infamous figures from the past –
such as William Shakespeare, Jesus,
Leonardo DaVinci, Julius Ceasar, or Tutankhamen –
but we do have representations of them
in the form of paintings, sculptures,
and a gold sarcophagus.
But who knows whether there are
visitors from the far future walking
the streets of the 21st Century
that can blend in so well
that they can pass us by
without us batting an eye.

There are things that we will never know
about what a place was really like way back when;
there are things that we will never know
about what certain people were really like
who are famous now but who were once
the child of a mother and a father;
there are things that we will never know
about what it must have been like
to see, to hear, to feel life on Earth
be remade repeatedly over the centuries.
There are things that we are only now discovering –
for example:
Did you know that some dinosaurs had feathers?

The Blessing

The beauty of the morning light
can often take your breath away...
the frigid conditions of a Winter's day
can often make you wish
that you could stay in bed...
the sound of the birds chirping in the trees
can make you feel hopeful and optimistic
for what might lie upon the path in front of you –
especially when you look around
at where you live, and you are captivated
by what you see on display...
for some people when they experience rubatosis –
the acute and often unsettling awareness
of their own heart beating in their chest –
it can make them think about and wonder
whether and when their mortal journey
will come to an end.

Every morning when I wake up
I open my eyes and I question
whether what I am looking at is real,
or whether I am still dreaming –
but it usually does not take me long
to realize that everything around me
is what is happening,
because if I were still dreaming
then I would be leaping around
in my mind to places, to times,
and to possibilities that I would
mostly be uncontrollable.

Whenever I have looked out
to the waves of an ocean,
or above to the stars of the night sky,
I have often been spellbound
and hypnotized by the fact
that no matter where I go and what I do
I cannot affect that which has been
in motion for longer than there
has been a Moon...
I have always loved the magic
of not knowing everything
and considering every day
the first step on an adventure
into the unknown as well as an exploration
into the depths of the familiar –
because I have always believed
that if given the gift to be able to learn
about somewhere, about something,
or about someone, what have we got to lose?

There is a reason why The Sun
and The Moon rise and set every day...
there is a reason why life is short
and why memories are important...
there is a reason why when we look
at something or someone we see them
as being beautiful, indescribable, special,
and a perpetual blessing.

Those Days

I can still remember those days
when it felt as if poetry
was flowing out of me
as easily as water falling
from the spout of a tap...
I can still remember those days
when the possibilities of life
felt so open I did not consider
that I might already
have been walking a particular path...
I can still remember those days
when everything I saw
and everything I felt
instantly inspired me
to write about them...
I can still remember those days
when I felt as if could not discern
whether my pen was driving me
or whether I was driving my pen...
I can still remember the feeling
of freedom and elation
that made me dream at night,
and sometimes during the day,
about indescribable and amazing
things that to this day
I would find it hard to put into words...
I can still remember those days
when everything that occurred to me
felt like the key to a door
that led to a brand-new world...

I can still remember those days
when I felt unbound and able
to believe anything was realizable
if I put my mind to it...
I can still remember those days
when I was still a tentative poet
that had so much to say,
who wrote all the time,
but who did not know
the right place to convey, to display,
to share, and to bridge the gap
between the stream of consciousness
that constantly flowed
like a torrent within his mind
and the ever-fertile blank page...
ten years ago –
those were the days.

Changing Voices

The voice of a writer, an artist,
a singer, a director, or a storyteller
naturally changes over the course of their career, because,
like every muscle that anyone uses regularly,
the more that someone uses
their gift of experience and imagination
the more that they can act, articulate, show,
or say something without
even having to think that much about it –
because over time some things become effortless
and, as a result, can grow
and to morph into a state of being
able to reform into any vision or personification
of anything or anyone imaginable.
The voice of people slowly but surely
gets deeper as they grow older...
the voice of people mostly gets wiser as they mature...
the voice of a person's internal dialogue
with themselves can get more insightful
when attempting to answer life-long
questions of meaning, reason, and choice...
the way that people communicate
with one another has been evolving
since our ancestors used to spend
their time sitting around a fire
while sharing their beliefs and opinions
about what they saw above them
when they looked up at the night sky,
as well as wondering what or who
created them and everything –
so it should be of no surprise for anyone
that everybody, over the course of their life,
will experience what it is like
to hear their own voice changing.

When Hope Eclipses Fear

The other night the Wolf Moon shone
big and bright in the sky...
last night, before darkness fell, the evening sky looked
as if it had been painted purple...
this morning, the bright white moon
continued to be a spectacle to behold long after sunrise.
However, for some reason, the Moon
looked more distant from Earth than it
had been just two days ago –
and it was at that moment that I realized
that Winter had officially arrived.

You can never truly know
what will happen during the season of Winter –
other than it will be cold, it will be wet,
and occasionally it will be freezing
and naturally slippery under foot...
you can never truly predict
how the elements will affect you,
nor how testing time will be...
you can never truly know
what to do, what to eat, nor what to wear –
other than to make sure that
you keep warm and think even more about
the needs and the well-being of those you love...
you can never truly predict what the conditions
of an average Winter day will be –
but you should anticipate
that certain things might take longer to do,
you should remember to not take anything for granted,
and if you must travel somewhere
you should consider whether
you have everything that you need
to get you from point A to point B.

Winter can be full
of a spectrum of moments –
ranging from the stark white
of a fresh snowfall
to the spectacular golden light
of a sunrise or a sunset...
Winter can be full of beautiful stillness,
especially at twilight,
when the stars at night shine brighter than
at any other time of the year...
Winter can be full of many colours,
stories, and surprises that find a way
of highlighting why for many reasons
Winter is when we see people at their best...
Winter can be full of uncertainty –
but with the help of those who
truly make a difference
and who matter the most
Winter can be the season when
hope eclipses fear.

Subculture

It has always fascinated me how,
no matter what century it is,
the various ages of culture
ultimately give rise to subcultures
of people who all walk to
the same beat of the same drum...
it has always been a source of inspiration
for me how on some level
everybody is always looking for a group
of like-minded individuals
who talk the same way, who dress the same way,
and who feel the same way about things,
about the world, about how they have
for so long been misunderstood –
and what brings them the most joy
in the world most likely does not
fit into the same mold of what is
considered to be mainstream or "normal".
It has always interested me
how easily people feel as if they
can be themselves when they are
given the opportunity to visit a place
which is sacred to them and safe for them
to indulge themselves in the conventions
of the subculture that they are
a practicing member of,
that are so iconic and expected
they have over time become a stereotype...
it has always given me a sense of acceptance
every time I have looked around the world
and without even having to try
I have been able to recognize
the unmistakable signs that point towards
someone who I might not know,
and who does not know me,

but who I may share similar sensibilities with,
who do not spend any effort or time
in disguising the fact that when it comes
to the road of life they are constantly walking a thin line.
It has always been a way of life
for the young of a society
to rebel against the rules of their parents
and thumb their nose at authority figures
to test the limits of what they can do,
to make their voice be heard.
However, sometimes when a certain
group of people feel as if they are being
unduly silenced then speech can slowly
transform into acts of delinquency,
disrespect, and disorder.
It will always be the case
that some people will want to believe
certain individual beliefs...
some people will always want to live a certain way of life...
some people will always want to act upon their instincts
and express what is meaningful to them –
because some things, to some people,
feel so indelible they are indistinguishable from their nature.
It goes without saying that normality
is a matter of opinion and perspective –
and where some may look at a group
of people and consider them to
have nothing constructive to offer
others might look at those same people
in the same way that they would look
at a family member,
because to them they are an example
of how an idea can grow and endure
under the radar as a subculture.

In Spirit

Sometimes we cannot be where we are supposed to be...
sometimes we find ourselves living at a distance from
those who we share a connection with...
sometimes we cannot reach out
and touch someone physically...
sometimes all we can do is use our voice,
while relying in-part upon the previous impression
that we made once before,
to give someone a feeling that,
though miles might separate,
strong and unbreakable bonds
between multiple individuals
can and do exist that can go on to flourish...
sometimes outside forces dictate
what our actions should be...
sometimes invisible adversaries infiltrate
and can disrupt the balance of calm...
sometimes people are unable to say
goodbye to people how, when, and where
they would prefer and have had to do so
virtually and in their own way...
it is sometimes torturous not knowing
when, where, or if you will ever see
someone you love again –
especially someone who has been
with you through so much and who perhaps in the past
was able to keep you from going off the deep end.
Sometimes we all wish we could
turn back the clock, go back in time,
and talk to someone who unfortunately we are
no longer in contact with –
someone who will always have
a presence is our lives,
even if, at this point, it is only in spirit.

Opening-up

Opening-up is not always easy...
being honest about your feelings
is not always as simple as it sounds...
speaking freely is not always
as easy as it should be...
telling someone what they want to hear
might be the right thing for you
to do in the short term,
but as time goes on that same person
may need to be gently coerced
into changing their ways
to turn their life around –
because people sometimes feel caged,
people sometimes feel trapped,
people sometimes feel silently enraged,
people sometimes feel as if they
are on a journey to somewhere
they know they want to go
but they do not know the right path to walk,
nor do they have any sort of a map.

Discovering that we are somehow different,
but at the same time living a life in parallel
to someone else, can be both confusing
and exciting at the same time...
further exploration of what we feel
we know about ourselves can be like
having a revelation that changes
everything about the world
that you thought you already knew:
a lie can become the truth,
and the truth can become a lie.

Knowing how, when, where,
and to whom to open-up to
can be like trying to cross a minefield –
because some people are more accepting
about certain things than others are...
knowing how and what to say
as accurately as possible
what you may have been mulling over
for what feels like your entire life
is sometimes something that must
to be rehearsed in front of a mirror...
it can sometimes be easier to tell
a stranger your innermost secrets
than it can be to expose yourself
to those who have known you the longest –
because there is something about
talking to someone who you
do not even know the name of
that can make it easier
for you to open-up.

The Candle

It is sometimes hard to know what to say,
it's sometimes hard to know what to do,
it's sometimes hard to know what someone
is personally going through
after they lose someone that they spent time with,
someone who they cared about,
someone who they loved,
and someone who they could never foresee
living in a world without;
but that is the anguish and that is the reality
of life and death that we all must sometimes grapple with –
which can make us all feel mentally lost,
physically sick, and emotionally devastated.
It is sometimes hard to put into words
what someone meant to you –
because usually there are too many
memories and too many experiences to look back on
and recount in every detail of what happened, when, why,
and how a particular person made us feel.
It's sometimes hard to know
if you have done enough for someone in need –
family members, friends, even strangers
who you can see are struggling with
a deep and excruciating pain;
but if you genuinely want to do something
for someone, then be there for them –
even if by doing so you are simply
on the other end of a phone,
grieving with them, giving them your time,
as well as the gift of your condolences
that are genuine, meaningful, and meant to help –
like the simple act of kindness
of remembering someone special
by lighting a candle.

David Bowie

Over the course of his life
he excited, he electrified, he entertained,
and he enriched the world through
his gift of creating art and music
that instantly struck and stayed
in the heart and in the minds of people,
like a bolt of lightning from the sky,
that made people feel, think,
and imagine things that they
may never have felt, thought,
nor dreamt of before.

He had a voice, he had a spirit,
he had a charm, a charisma, a presence
that could immediately captivate
crowds of fans and made them want
to sing and dance and lift up
their eyes and their hands,
because he was able to make
people feel as if they
could reach out and touch
the energy of a star
that could inspire them with a purpose,
that was able to show just how varied
and full of colour each of us are –
and to this day he and his music
makes us consider a variety of possibilities:
including whether there really is
Life on Mars?

He was a man who was not afraid of change,
nor of changing his identity
and how he was perceived...
he was a man who was not afraid
of experimentation
nor of collaboration with fellow artists
who he connected with and felt as if
they understood him
and spoke the language of magic,
imagination and inspiration that he did.

He was a hero, and he still is...
he was, he is, and he always will be
an icon and a god of music in the eyes
of millions of people around the world –
and who he was and what he did
was all that he ever wanted to be:
a man who transcended
but who was also connected to the world,
a man who left an indelible legacy,
a man who gave us all a part of his soul
to remember him by,
a man who had he not died would
today have celebrated turning 75,
a man whose face we will forever see,
a man whose songs will be listened to
by generation after generation on repeat:
the man, the legend,
the one and the only
David Bowie.

The Horizon

Last night the sky was clear,
the air outside was inviting,
and The Moon was shining bright,
as people from all around the world
bid farewell to the year before
and welcomed the arrival
of the year to come with excitement,
with high spirits, with hope,
with messages of love,
with embraces, with kisses, and with cheer.

Today, after the chimes
of the bells that ushered in
a brand-new orbit around the sun have quietened,
there is a palpable feeling
of unbridled bewilderment –
because it feels as if now, more than ever,
no one knows what will happen next,
nor what twists and turns
the people of the world can expect.

The last 12 months have been
unlike any other in recorded history –
because over the last 365 days
there have been moments when
people have literally found themselves
catching their breath while wondering
when life will go back to how it used to be.

Last night,
at the arrival of a new day,
as the fireworks were launched
into the darkness of the night
to enlighten the eyes
and the dreams of many,
one year became another,
and, for a moment,
time felt as if it had stopped
and there was a wave of connection
that engulfed everyone –
one that began long before,
intending to deliver the possibility
of a new beginning to anyone who wants one.

The first day of the year
is something special –
because, no matter what happened before
and no matter what happens after,
everybody can take a step back
while they take a step forward
to discover what awaits them,
like the light of a new day,
just over the horizon.

Angels of Salvation

Today is a day for fireworks!
Today is a time for celebration!
Now is a time when people
around the world gather,
make plans, feel thankful,
and once again hold hands –
and it is at this time of the year
when the days are short
and when daylight is precious,
when people brave the cold
and follow the lights that they see,
as they venture out into the dark
to find and discover seasonal treats
that always bring people
some much-needed joy to their life
and make both adults and children laugh.

Today, now, any day, any time,
is always the right day and the right time
to reach out and tell someone
what they mean to you
and give them the gift of explaining to them
what they have that no one else has...
today, every day, someone you know
might need you more than you know –
and all that they need is someone, anyone,
to tell them that if they need someone
to speak to about how they feel
about anything, they have you –
and to some people that is like the feeling
of elation and salvation that the survivor
of a sunken ship feels after they
once again finally find dry land.

Today, every day, for most people,
can be like undertaking an uphill struggle
and not knowing what they will find
when they finally reach the top –
which is why friends, coworkers,
family members, forgotten acquaintances,
even blink and you miss them
strangers who might you see
on the street are important,
because they have the power to give
everyone who needs it the fuel,
the spark, the energy, the boost
to light up someone's sky and remind
everybody who needs to be reminded
that all is never always lost
and there are heroes out there
in the world who will do what they can,
when they can, for whomever they can,
no matter the cost, and who will gladly sacrifice
what they must to throw an arm of comfort
around those who feel as if they have
no one to turn to and nowhere else to go –
and those people are true
Angels of Salvation.

Zen

For there to be white,
there must and black...
for there to be light,
there must be dark...
for there to yin
there must be a yang...
for there to be stars, heat,
and life on any given planet,
there must be the cold and hostile
vacuum of space for the two opposing
forces of nature – life and death –
to have their way and test the limits
and the extremes of their own potential.
For good to prevail
there must be evil to vanquish...
for hope to win in the end
there must be the shadow of doubt
to sometimes struggle with...
for the best of the best to be crowned
there must be ups and downs
from which lessons are learned
which inspire others down the road
who are on their own journey of self-discovery.
For the entirety of this version of the universe
there has existed both
the beginning and the end,
the start and the finish,
the Go and the Stop,
the found and the lost –
but there are places where and when
the interconnected consciousness
of all living things communicates
with one another consciously
as well as unconsciously,

that some have even reported
to have visited and returned from
feeling changed and brand new:
nirvana, heaven, Eden,
space, the frontier, the edge,
high above the clouds
or deep below the ocean –
after which they can both perceive
and understand forever that
the balance that keeps the wheels
of existence rolling as serenely
as a sphere of energy
spinning through space,
that is both perfect
and imperfect at the same time,
would have to be one of the most
wonderful symbols in existence
that captures the true essence
of what it means to be
Zen.

The Evening Sky

Against the blue and gold hue of the sky,
at sunset I watch the silhouette of
a flock of birds fly across the sky,
as the daylight drains away
and darkness rises...
the moments of twilight are so beautiful
that I cannot look away,
because I am always entranced
by the transition between the world
of day and the world of night...
there has always been something
magical to me about sitting
in the dark, while watching and waiting
for the clouds to clear and the divine
light of the stars to pierce through the vastness –
like some kind of celestial knives.

I love living where I live –
in the countryside and away
from the city sights and sounds –
because I can be inspired
by nature, up close and personal,
and every day and every night
look up to the sky and feel as if
I can see the face of heaven
looking back at me, perfect and bright,
at the same time gifting me
a vision and some sort of second sight
that makes me feel like
a shooting star arching from left to right
unimpeded through the evening sky.

Back to the Theatre

Finally, I am back in the seat
of a cinema, sitting in the dim light,
and waiting patiently for the room
to go dark and the film that I am
here to see to start.

It has been a long time since
I was able to embrace my cinephile side
and get back to where I always looked
forward to returning to every so often...
it has been a long time since
anybody who loves the magic
and the experience of seeing a film
on the biggest screen there is
has been able to go to the movies,
to perhaps get some popcorn and a cold drink,
sit in a comfortable seat,
and switch off from the world
while they are transported away
to a place of fiction and fantasy,
and embrace the gift and the opportunity
of pure, unadulterated, escapism.

I am a dreamer, I am an artist,
and I am also someone
who loves enjoying the labor
of other people's imagination and creativity...
since I was a child, I have always been
someone who loves going to the cinema –
because I have always understood
the language and the power
of visual and auditory storytelling,
and the way that subtleties
in colour and sound can feed the mind,
as well as revitalize and influence
the thoughts, the feelings, and the emotions
of people young and old far into the future.

I don't see every film at the cinema,
but when I see the trailer for an
upcoming film that immediately
grabs my attention,
I try to make the time,
when the film is finally released,
to see it in a place where I can
make the most of every moment
of movie making poetry –
which is why I am so happy,
which is why I am so energized,
and which is why I am so in awe
to once again be back enjoying a movie
projected upon the screen within a theatre.

The Best of Us

Each of us can find contentment
doing things that make us happy...
each of us can find hidden secrets
about life, about people,
about every-day things or situations
that can make us all take another look
at the world, and at ourselves,
and allow us to realize that there
is more seemingly "small things" –
simple gestures, simple tokens –
that mean the most in the long run
and down the line when a smile
on a face is all that we crave.

Each of us need things to explore...
each of us need one another...
each of us need both windows and doors...
each of us need the feeling of being
included and not excluded from
what is going on in the world,
in the galaxy, in the quest of humanity
and all life everywhere to find the next
check point on the journey
that is their purpose –
whether that is to be found in a forest,
on a mountain top, above the clouds,
or below the waves on the seafloor.

Each of us can do extraordinary things –
even if we might not initially
recognize our gifts for being as profound
and as impactful as they are...

each of us make mistakes,
each of us do things that we regret,
because each of us are human –
and I believe our failings should not
forever be considered mortal sins
by some from which we can
not move on from, learn from,
and change as a result.

Each of us are a miracle – warts and all...
each of us are soulful individuals
who over our life will feel feelings
and emotions from love to guilt;
but, to me, the spectrum of what
people are capable of symbolizes
everything about life that nobody
can do anything about:
some things just are what they are,
just as each of us are
who and what we are
and have always been
destined to be since birth –
as were, and as will always be,
the best of us.

The Runners and Riders

Every weekend
within the village where I live,
there is a convergence, a meeting,
a gathering of runners and riders
who, for some reason, feel drawn
to my home's crossroads
of paths and directions…
every weekend
people of every walk of life
set out of their homes
and eventually find themselves
at the same place, at the same time,
marveling at the journey they took
to be where they are and sharing
within their conversations their
mutual appreciation of what
always makes their thoughts race
and their heart beat faster and faster.

I, myself, am a walker…
I, myself, like to stop and literally smell the roses…
I, myself, am a daydreamer…
I, myself, like to be unbounded to idea
of exactly where I am going
and let fate take me where and when it chooses.

I have been both a runner
and a rider in my time –
and I can still recall the exhilaration
that I used to feel every time
that I pushed my body to the limit
while I got to where I needed –
however, nowadays, I am more of a free spirit
who goes with the flow.

I have been someone
who has had near misses –
and if the universe had had other
plans for me then I would not
be talking to you now…
I do not know how to be any different
than who I have become as a result
of all my experiences and adventures
that I have had over my life –
every so often dancing with
the flames of fate's fire –
which is why I always feel
a genuine kinship with all of life's
many and varied runners and riders.

Why?

There is always a reason,
there is always a why,
there is always a motivation
for the myriad of actions
that people sometimes take,
and for the many decisions
that people sometimes make,
that they have no trouble in
being able to justify.

Where there is a spark
there will always be a flame...
where there is touch and proximity
there will always be intimacy...
where there is language
there is will always be consideration,
interpretation and loss –
because truth and reality
are not always the same...
where there is the evidence of stories
of the past there will always remain mysteries.

Myths, legacies, stories, records,
chronicles, cave paintings, rock carvings
are important depictions of a mixture
of both fiction and fact all rolled into one...
sometimes it does not take anything more
than someone saying that they heard
a voice tell them to do something
for them to immediately act
seemingly without thinking,
nor without a fight.

Symbols, signs, warnings, lessons,
cautionary tales are vital for
any civilization to learn the merits
of what is right and what is wrong...
sometimes it takes the bravest of the brave
to stop something that they know
is going to happen before it happens –
so that someday someone will not have to
look back upon a choice that they made
and must justify to others,
and perhaps to themselves,
the answer to the question:
why?

A Light in the Dark

After the sun had set,
as the sky above looked
a darker blue than black,
I saw a lone star shining
its light down upon me,
and I began to feel out of breath...
as I continued to stare at the star,
I did what came naturally:
I wished that my Dad were still with us
and I hoped that he was proud of me.

Every time I look up at the sky
and I see The Moon and the stars,
I am reminded every single time
that every one of us
are a part of something bigger...
every time I am sitting or standing in silence,
I never for a second feel alone –
because even though I do not
see anybody else around me
I know that I am being watched over
by a guiding light whose shine,
even in twilight,
could not be brighter.

As the light dims further,
more stars of the galaxy
begin to show themselves...
as darkness consumes the world
I can feel my heart beating in my chest,
and as I close my eyes,
as I reach out with my mind,
I can sense a connection
that I have always known
and I have always felt.

Every time I remember the past
I hear my Dad's voice
giving me the answer to a question
that only now I am ready to truly ask:
"Who am I? Where am I going?"
And I hear my Dad say to me:
"You are who you have always been to me.
You are my son, Mark...
You shine brighter than any other,
because you are a light in the dark".

The Comeback Kid

He had been hurt...
He had been cursed...
He had learned the hard way
that some things are not meant to last –
but people who truly knew Him
always believed and expected
that He would one day make a comeback...
He had felt turned inside-out...
He had felt used and worn-out...
He had been attacked on every side,
He had been thought to have been defeated,
He had been left wounded
and scarred from His experiences –
but the people who had thought Him
easily destroyed always got a shock
when He rose again like The Sun
and found a way to close the distances.

Some people would rather discount fate
and mistakenly believe that life is all a series of coincidences,
but His interactions had taught Him otherwise –
which is why He was always trusting His senses.

He had been deceived...
He had been non-believed...
He had been thrown to the side
like a piece of litter from a car window –
but what some people do not know, or realize,
is that He never forgets, and He always remembers,
everything and every face
that He has been shown.

He has spoken…
He has listened…
He has been broken…
He has been awakened
to the good and the bad
of what others and He himself did…
He has felt burned –
physically, as well as in effigy;
but, do you know what?
He does not regret the fact
that He has lived.

He is many things,
but one thing that He likes about himself,
and what some people have said
that they admire about Him,
is that, no matter what happens,
He will always return,
and He will always rise
like a phoenix from the flames –
because He will always be
"The Comeback Kid":
Me, myself, and I.

MARK HASTINGS

Mark's other poetry collections:
Poet of the Sphere
The Sound of Mark
The Eternal Boy
The Dreamer and The Dream
Too Close To The Sun
The Rambler
Poet of the Multiverse
Which are all available as an eBook or in Paperback at:
Amazon.com
Amazon.co.uk

Printed in Great Britain
by Amazon